T0146533

Swan's
SOUP
&
Salad

Swan's SOUP & *Salad*

Humorous Stories That Nourish the Heart

DR. DENNIS SWANBERG

HOWARD
PUBLISHING CO.

Our purpose at Howard Publishing is to:

- *Increase faith* in the hearts of growing Christians
- *Inspire holiness* in the lives of believers
- *Instill hope* in the hearts of struggling people
  everywhere

Because He's coming again!

Swan's Soup and Salad © 1999 by Dennis Swanberg
All rights reserved. Printed in the United States of America

Published by Howard Publishing Co., Inc.,
3117 North 7th Street, West Monroe, Louisiana 71291-2227

03 04 05 06 07 08   10 9 8 7 6 5

Library of Congress Cataloging-in-Publication Data

Swanberg, Dennis, 1953–
        Swan's soup and salad : humorous stories that nourish the heart / Dennis Swanberg
          p. cm.
        ISBN 1-58229-013-X
        1. Christian life Anecdotes.   I. Title.
BV4517.S93   1999
242—dc21   99-29532
                                                                                     CIP

Illustrations by Hamp Law
Edited by Jennifer Stair and Janet Reed
Interior Design by Stephanie Denney

TABLE OF CONTENTS

SPECIAL THANKS

The list of people who have stood behind me and encouraged me as I have tried to encourage others is endless. Here, I want to thank some of those special loved ones who have tolerated and participated in my frequent servings of stories and antics.

Floyd Leon and Pauline Bernadeen Swanberg have endured a steady diet of their son for over four decades without much variety in the menu. Sisters Darlene Simril and Teri Tidmore have sat at "life's table" of humor with their brother for many a meal.

In-laws, George and Kathy Wilkes have survived many "luncheon specials" and "midnight snack" routines and are to be commended for accommodating such clowning cholesterol in their son-in-law!

Special praises go to my wife, Lauree, who deserves at least one seven-course meal without the Swan's side orders of humor, but who has never complained about the entrées her Swan delivers day after day.

And thanks to my boys, Chad and Dusty, for their willingness to "consume" what their dad dishes out, even his humor, all for the cause of Christ and his Kingdom work through laughter. The boys have known the cafeteria lines of comedy their whole lives, and yet they still enjoy their dad. Thanks, boys!

And thanks to all the churches that have allowed the Swan to encourage their saints. For over twenty-three years, I have served local churches, and it was in these churches that I learned how to laugh—at myself and with the body of Christ. I learned that life is too short not to enjoy—or, as some would say, too long not to enjoy.

I want to thank all the believers who have stood with me in my Ministry of Encouragement. Steve and Ann Cretin, John and Selene Rea, Joe and Robin Thomas, Pat and Ann Williams, Rick and Tracey Lineberger, Bruce and Cindy Edwards, and Benji and Connie Harlan. The "Steel Magnolias" and their husbands: Judy and Jerry Foster, Debra and Mark Hendricks, Brenda and Tony Davis, and Shirley and Mark Pilcher have been constant companions of faith and fun.

A special thanks goes to two former teenagers who were in my youth ministry in the early seventies, Sam and Barbara Cox Maley. Sam and Barbara eventually fell in love, got married, and now support the Swan prayerfully and financially in his Ministry of Encouragement. They were two of the first to support the idea for this book. Thanks for believing in me, Sam and Barbara!

I want to give a Big Swan thank you to Hamp Law for his creativity in creating cartoons that capture the "lighter side" of each chapter. "Hamp, you the man!" Hamp has known the Swan as pastor, preacher, and friend. Thanks for teaming up with me on my "low fat" buffet of laughter. It's not only a good meal...it's healthy like a medicine.

I could go on and on, but I'll stop now by saying thanks most of all to our Lord, from whom all blessings flow!

INTRODUCTION

If you're like me, you love to eat out. I especially like to eat at those all-you-can-eat, serve-yourself places. My favorite buffet food is meat and taters. But of course my wife, Lauree (alias Honey Love and Sugar Babe), wants me to eat more soup and salad so I won't literally "fill the pulpit" when I speak and entertain. I'm learning that balance is the key. Too much heavy food slows me down, bloats me up, and gives me indigestion.

We all need balance in our spiritual diet as well. A constant diet of heavy, scholarly reading might give us a case of "spiritual indigestion." Sometimes we need something light, yet filling. And that's why I've written *Swan's Soup and Salad*. In the midst of life's buffet of choices, we need to sometimes choose the soup-and-salad bar for appropriate helpings of lighthearted laughter and encouragement. And we all need an occasional side salad of sidesplitting laughter and a blessed bowl of bountiful joy.

Storytelling is my way of serving up spiritual soup and salad. Jesus was a storyteller too. He often "spake a parable" (told a story) to his friends and followers. Storytelling allows life's incredible authenticities to be told with a flair for the funny and a tribute to the truth. Stories draw us close to the master storyteller and allow us to see ourselves as he sees us—with a grin, a chuckle, and much love.

As you read, you need to know that some of my stories have not been changed in order to protect the innocent. Others have undergone ministerial license and energized embellishment.

It is my prayer that this book will offer you a smorgasbord of fun food for thought and delightful dishes for spiritual nourishment. And it's the desire of "Chef Swan" that each chapter nourish your heart and tantalize your spiritual taste buds with "bacon bits"of truth, "croutons" of comfort, and servings of substance—leaving you served and satisfied.

Part One

GROWING UP ON FUN

"Look, Floyd, look. Would you just look at that woman in red. Oh my!"

GROWING UP ON FREE FUN

I have a great mom, Pauline Bernadeen, and dad, Floyd Leon, and I'm thankful for my mama and daddy. Now, those really are their names: Floyd Leon (he's six-feet-two-inches tall) and Pauline Bernadeen (she's only five feet tall). I thank God every day that I'm named Dennis. Let me tell you why.

My grandpa's name was Elof. He came from Sweden to Texas when he was only fourteen. My grandma's name was Agda. I also had an Uncle Ungvi, an Uncle Turi, and an Aunt Signi in my family. Now can you see why every day of my life I thank God that my name is Dennis?

We Swanbergs are just regular folks. When I was growing up, we didn't always have a whole bunch of money, but that was all right. We learned to do things that were fun but didn't cost us anything.

For example, we'd load up the family in our '49 Ford and drive from our country town down to Congress Avenue, the main street of Austin, Texas. Then we'd park in front of the Paramount Theater. We never went to the movie; we just watched the people lined up to go. It didn't cost us a thing. People would line up to buy their tickets, go in, and come out—and we'd just watch.

I remember how closely my mama and daddy would watch—especially my mama, Pauline Bernadeen. She would sit there on the front seat and lean up next to Floyd—they were still in that stage of life where they liked to be close together. My older sister, Sherry Darlene, and I would sit in the back seat. (My little sister, Teri Linn, wasn't born yet.) Pauline would snuggle close to Floyd, and he'd put his arm around her. They would just look at people and have the time of their lives.

Once Mama said, "Look, Floyd, look. Would you just look at that woman? That woman in red, behind the man in the blue. Look what she has on. Can you believe she's wearing that? Could you imagine if I wore something like that? Oh my!"

I remember my daddy watching that woman walk all the way down the sidewalk. Then he looked at us kids, shaking his head sadly, and said, "Isn't that pitiful? Now that *is* pitiful." Of course, Daddy was a deacon, so he was especially picky about what people wore.

Sometimes we'd drive over to Robert Mueller Airport and do the same thing. We'd watch people get on and off the planes. We never flew in a plane, but we enjoyed just watching people get on and off and watching the planes take off and land.

I remember one time a whole family of five came off a plane. Old Floyd Leon, watching them, smacked his forehead in disbelief. "Good night, looky there! A family of five. That is ridiculous. Lord have mercy. One of them could have gone and come back and told the rest of them all about it."

We kids spent a lot of time at the automatic doors. The airport had just put in some pressure-sensitive rubber mats. When you stepped on the rubber mats, the glass door automatically opened. My sister and I could play on that thing for hours. Now I was raised a Methodist, so I knew how to shake a leg. I would just get a goin', and I'd get that door a goin' until old Floyd Leon would come over and say, "All right, get on off there now. Let some other kids play on it for a while." That was the closest we ever came to Six Flags over Texas.

I learned an important lesson from Daddy and Mama when I was young; I learned how to be happy, even when we didn't have everything we ever wanted.

FOOD FOR THOUGHT
I have learned in whatever state I am, to be content.
—Philippians 4:11

The apostle Paul wrote to his beloved church at Philippi, "I have learned in whatever state I am, to be content: I know how to be abased, and I know how to abound. Everywhere and in all things I have learned both to be full and to be hungry, both to abound and to suffer need" (Philippians 4:11–12). What is remarkable is that Paul was a prisoner in Rome when he wrote these words. He was on trial for his life. Paul understood that he could have plenty or little and that he could be content with either.

Bill Gates, who is worth thirty-seven billion dollars and rising, has a sixty-million-dollar home that took seven years to build. It is a "smart house" with every conceivable electronic device. Yet I am certain that Bill Gates is not more content in his multimillion-dollar "smart house" than I was in our happy home in Austin. There is absolutely no evidence that complexity and materialism lead to happiness. On the contrary, there is plenty of evidence that simplicity and spirituality lead to joy, a blessedness that is better than happiness.

Sometimes the people who appear the happiest are the least content. In the earliest days of Freudian psychiatry, a very depressed man sat in the office of a London psychiatrist. The doctor could do nothing to cheer the man up. Finally he gave up and suggested to his patient, "Why don't you go see Grimaldi the clown?" Grimaldi was the greatest clown in nineteenth-century Europe; surely he could lift this man's spirits.

The patient sighed and remained silent for a long time. Finally he answered, "I *am* Grimaldi the clown."

True happiness and contentment cannot come from the things of this world. The blessedness of true joy is a free gift that comes only from our Lord and Savior, Jesus Christ.

"Dennis, get that thing off his tongue right now. No telling how many other people have had it on their tongues."

FUNERAL-HOME
FANS AND TONGUE
DEPRESSORS

I grew up attending a little Swedish Methodist church in the country. During the services, I'd sit in the back pew with my buddies and have a good time. We tried to pay attention, but sometimes it was hard. Even though we had a great preacher, my heart just wasn't always into the sermon. Sometimes I took a bulletin and filled in the Os and the Bs and the Ds. (Tell the truth and shame the devil—you've done it too!)

We didn't always have bulletins, though, in that little church outside of Austin. But we always had funeral-home fans. Thank God for the funeral home that provided us with those fans. We'd just fan ourselves like crazy, and that would give us something to do. On one side of the fan was a picture of Jesus praying on a rock or knocking on a door. On the other side was the funeral home's advertisement displaying different kinds of caskets, types of metal, and things like that. A local doctor had donated some tongue depressors for us to staple onto the fans so they'd have handles.

I can remember taking a tongue depressor stapled to a fan and using it to "examine" an unwitting friend. The man behind us scolded, "Dennis, get that thing off his tongue right now. No telling how many other people have had it on their tongues." Of course, back then I didn't worry about germs or diseases like we do nowadays.

As I recall, we Methodists just used one staple in our tongue depressors because we were methodical and steady right down the line. My Baptist buddies usually used two staples to keep their fans attached because they got sort of excited during their occasional week-long revivals. And if a lady in the Baptist choir ever got upset about not being picked to sing a solo, it sort of helped to have two staples in her fan. My Pentecostal and charismatic friends usually needed three staples in their tongue depressors because they always got excited, and they tended to throw their fans across the room in moments of joy.

FOOD FOR THOUGHT

The things which are seen are temporary,
but the things which are not seen are eternal.

—2 Corinthians 4:18

Funeral-home fans remind me how quickly once-common things can pass away. Just a generation ago, everyone knew what a funeral-home fan was. Nowadays you'd be hard-pressed to find a Gen-Xer who has ever seen one. But that's not too surprising. The things that impress people so much today will be gone tomorrow. Paul expressed it this way: "We do not look at the things which are seen, but at the things which are not seen. For the things which are seen are temporary, but the things which are not seen are eternal" (2 Corinthians 4:18).

Here's a simple test: If you can see it, it's not going to last. The only things left from the physical world of Paul's day are ruins, and most of them have already been dug up. The mighty Roman military, senate, culture, and empire are all long gone. The same thing is going to happen to us one day. Look around you. Although the things you see might look like pretty sturdy stuff, you can write over all of them with a single word: *Disappearing.*

The things that last are the things you cannot see. The love of God lasts. Faith lasts. Hope lasts. The very essence of the Christian faith belongs to the future and the invisible. That is the meaning of the great definition of faith: "Now faith is the substance of things hoped for [the future], the evidence of things not seen [the invisible]" (Hebrews 11:1).

Funeral-home fans, rock stars, skyscrapers, and high-tech industries—one day, they will all disappear. Think about this: One of the biggest businesses of the nineteenth century made buggy whips. How many people today have ever seen a buggy whip? You can be sure that our advanced computers will be the buggy whips of the next century. Only the things that belong to God will last. The problem with some people is that they wed themselves to a disappearing order. You may like the flash of the world's parade, but if you look down the street, you can see that the parade will eventually come to an end.

In contrast to the temporary things of this world, consider the words of Isaiah 40:8: "The grass withers, the flower fades, but the word of our God stands forever." You never can get away from God's Word. In recent years, our culture has experienced an explosion of interest about the Bible. Recently, Bill Moyers hosted one of the most heralded PBS series ever, focused on the Book of Genesis. *The Bible Code*, a best-selling book, is an incredible examination of secret messages alleged to be in the Bible. People are desperate to find something that will last, and they are seeking the truth of God's Word.

A city slicker once watched an old country blacksmith swinging his hammer. He observed, "You must have worn out a lot of anvils."

The old blacksmith never stopped his work. As he slammed the hammer against the anvil again and again, he replied, "Nope. I've only had one anvil, but I've worn out hundreds of hammers."

Some people hammer away at the Word of God, thinking it will not last. But God's Word only wears out the hammers. It's the one thing that will last forever.

We'd heard about escalators; we'd read about escalators; but we'd never actually seen one.

Chapter

ESCALATOR
EXCITEMENT

When I was growing up, we found excitement in little things. On Friday and Saturday nights we'd walk out on the front porch and scan the skyline for floodlights. When we spotted light beams, we knew there was a grand opening somewhere in town. That meant free cokes and free hot dogs, and we wouldn't have to pay for supper that night.

I'll never forget the night when Montgomery Ward opened on I-35, right in the Capitol Plaza shopping center. It was a two-story building, and you know what that meant: On the inside of that building was an *escalator*. We were so excited. We'd heard about escalators; we'd read about escalators; but we'd never actually seen one.

By the time we got to Montgomery Ward, it was already crowded. My dad, Floyd Leon, didn't want us to get separated before we got to the escalator. He's a tough guy with an authoritative voice, and he barked out, "Everybody hold hands."

So we held hands. In fact, at my daddy's command, several other families also grabbed hands. My daddy had spent twenty-one years in the Thirty-Sixth Infantry Division of the National Guard in Austin, Texas. He retired as a major. He just has that kind of command about him.

We wandered through the store, holding hands, and finally found the escalator. Man, the stairs would disappear and then reappear, moving all the while—we just couldn't believe it. At first we just stood there and watched people riding on that thing. When I look back on it now, I know my daddy was nervous because this is the way he handled it: When it was our turn, he said to my little five-foot mama, Pauline Bernadeen, "Sugar babe, you go first, baby. Go ahead, honey. You go on. Step on up there, baby love. Don't be afraid, baby."

I know my daddy's blood pressure must have been topping the charts. He was scared, but he was also excited. It was exciting for all of us. Our first ride on a real, live *escalator*. First went Mama. Then went little sister, Teri Linn. Then big sister, Sherry Darlene. Then me. Floyd Leon came last. Next thing I knew, we were all on that escalator. Oh man, that was a fun time. We rode all the way up to the top.

I remember my dad said, "Let's do it one more time." So we rode that thing back down.

Then Mama and Daddy decided they'd go up to the top floor and look at the color televisions. I remember those color televisions—they were the circular kind. Only certain programs were in color back then, and they came on after the NBC "peacock" appeared on the screen.

My daddy saw those televisions from across the room and said, "There's a *peacock,* baby love." So my mama and daddy hooked 'em on over there. They wanted to see a color program on television. My sisters went with them, but I wanted to stay on that escalator just a little bit longer. I rode that thing up and down, up and down, and finally my daddy came and found me at the bottom. There I stood, just watching the handle go up and around, up and around.

You see, I had attention deficit disorder. Back then, we didn't have ritalin; kids with the disorder were just a riddle. No one even knew what to call it. Grownups just solved the problem by beating the tar out of the kid, you know what I mean? They just put him in the corner or in the hallway, and that was that.

Every year at school, I was always the fortunate one to get to sit right next to the teacher. The teacher would say, "Dennis, you're gonna put your desk right next to my desk and be my special helper this year."

I'd say, "Great! That's what I did last year."

Every year, I was the teacher's special helper. I didn't know that I was really the one who needed the help. I thought I was being rewarded.

So there I was, watching the handle go around and around on that escalator. The next thing I knew, my daddy came up and said, "Good night, son, what in the world are you doin'?"

And I said, "Waitin' for my gum." Then I spotted a little pink wad coming toward me. "Yonder it comes!" And it did! It came back around on that escalator handle, and I got my gum back!

FOOD FOR THOUGHT

*Cast your bread upon the waters,
for you will find it after many days.*
—Ecclesiastes 11:1

The gum-on-the-escalator incident reminds me of the old expression, "What goes around comes around." That somewhat cynical proverb is based on a fatalism about life. One of the great promises of the Bible is found in Psalm 103:10–11: "He has not dealt with us according to our sins, nor punished us according to our iniquities. For as the heavens are high above the earth, so great is His mercy toward those who fear Him."

That chewing gum came back around. Some fatalistic people cynically think life will always be like that—bad things will eventually come back to haunt the rest of your life. Not so, says God. God does not always let the consequences of our mistakes catch up with us. For the sake of Jesus Christ, God often stops the ultimate consequences of our sins. No, life is not always like an escalator that brings us back to the same place and keeps us from ever breaking out of the cycle.

But in another sense, what goes around does come around. When you launch an act of kindness out into the crosswinds of life, it will blow kindness back to you. When you act with generosity, you will get generosity in return. The author of Ecclesiastes was something of a cynic, but he affirmed this truth: "Cast your bread upon the waters, for you will find it after many days" (11:1). In the very best sense, what goes around does come around. An act of goodness comes back to us in the form of goodness. Although we sometimes think that our acts of patience, encouraging words, and quiet deeds of thoughtfulness have disappeared; they have not. They eventually come back around. Having blessed others, they bless us.

Scientists tell us that every word and picture ever broadcast electronically is still somewhere out in space, billions of miles away. If humans ever go to other planets, they may see an old episode of Gunsmoke. Amazing as that sounds, there is something even more astonishing: Not a single act of goodness in Jesus' name has ever disappeared. Every act of kindness reaches out and touches the lives of thousands of people—one at a time.

Indeed, in the very best sense, what goes around comes around.

When you've got attention
deficit disorder, you feel led
to do all kinds of things.

Chapter 4

NIP
IT IN THE
BUD

What goes on in church is often a mystery to little boys. The Swan is living proof of that.

One Sunday in our little Swedish Methodist church, the preacher was preachin', and he asked a rhetorical question. I was just a little fellow, six or seven years old. I didn't understand what a rhetorical question was.

The pastor asked dramatically, "What should we *do* with sin?" He was an old-time preacher who sounded like Dr. W. A. Criswell of First Baptist Church of Dallas.

Well, I was sitting in the back with my buddies. My mama and daddy were sitting up toward the front. I looked around and thought, *Why isn't anybody answering him? Man, a grownup*

ought to help this preacher. One of his own kind ought to come through for him.

No one did. My heart went out to the man, but I didn't want to say anything out loud. It wasn't proper to speak out loud in that particular church. So I just gestured to him and mouthed the words, "We don't know. We don't know."

The preacher did not pay any attention to me. Why should he? I was just a little fellow in the back. I was so small, he probably couldn't even see me trying to get his attention. He just kept right on preaching.

Sure enough, he repeated the question. The second time he sort of cried it out, "*What* should we *do* with *sin?*"

Once again, my little heart went out to him. I stood up this time, gestured with wider motions, and mouthed, "We don't know. I don't know. They don't know. You don't know. Only God knows. Don't ask us, ask him."

I was trying to help the man. I said to myself, *If he asks that question one more time, I am going to answer him out loud.* That's what I felt led to do. You know, when you've got attention deficit disorder, you feel led to do all kinds of things. I thought, *I will be a hero! I will help this man. I will give him an answer.*

You know what's coming, don't you? But when you've got that ADD problem as a little fellow, you think you're right on target. Though your actions aren't always appropriate, your heart is pure. (The Bible says in Matthew 5:8 that the pure in heart shall see God. When you do what I did, you may see him sooner than later.)

22

Sure enough, the preacher lowered his voice and dramatically whispered, "What should we do with sin?"

I just couldn't take it anymore. Someone had to answer this man. I stood up on the pew and, inspired by a phrase used by Barney Fife of *Andy Griffith,* I yelled, "Nip it in the bud! You gotta nip it in the bud!"

Well, people in that old Methodist church went almost charismatic. Senior adult ladies were screeching all around me. They could have died right there and gone on to glory. In the twinkling of an eye, I found myself sitting between Floyd Leon and Pauline Bernadeen. How I got there I don't know, but there I was.

FOOD FOR THOUGHT

But who do you say that I am?
—Matthew 16:15

Some people just don't understand rhetorical questions. Have you ever asked someone how his day was going and had him give you an answer longer than a Tom Clancy novel? Sometimes you ask questions as a formality, not because you want an answer. These questions are simply rhetorical.

Yet some questions are definitely *not* rhetorical. Some questions are so important that the answer literally means the difference between life and death. Six months before his crucifixion, the Lord Jesus took his disciples to a remote site in the far north of the Holy Land. There he asked them an important question: "Who do you say that I am?" (Matthew 16:15).

That's one question that you really cannot step over, around, or under. That's not a rhetorical question. He expects an answer from each of us.

Every church steeple asks that question. Every cross worn around a person's neck asks that question. All of the artistic masterpieces that picture Jesus Christ ask that question. Handel's *Messiah* asks that question. The greatest thinkers in Western civilization—Augustine, Luther, Calvin, Knox, Cromwell, and a thousand others like them—ask that question. Every document that has "A.D." on it asks that question. The architecture of the great cathedrals asks that question. It is the question of the ages: Who is Jesus Christ?

The great British scholar C. S. Lewis put it simply in his book *Mere Christianity:* Jesus Christ is either a liar, a lunatic, or Lord. Jesus Christ claimed to be the Son of God. If he claimed to be the Son of God and knew he was not, he was a liar. If Jesus Christ thought he was the Son of God but in reality was not, he was a lunatic. The only other option is that Jesus Christ actually was who he claimed to be—Lord of all.

The question about Jesus' true identity is not rhetorical; it is a question that every person must answer. Who do you say that Jesus is?

The only adequate answer is the one given by Simon Peter: "You are the Christ, the Son of the living God" (Matthew 16:16). If you are considering any other response, you need to nip it in the bud!

Daddy was the kind of man who could discipline you and then immediately fellowship with you.

SOFTBALL NIGHTS

Discipline has changed considerably since I was a boy. Today parents debate over what kind of verbal discipline to give their kids so they don't damage their kids' self-esteem. Not long ago, parents debated whether to use physical or verbal discipline on their children. When I was growing up, my parents didn't have any such concerns. Their only debate was whether I got whomped right then or later that night. Today many parents just send Junior to his room. Big deal. In his room, Junior has every known video game, a television with cable, the Internet, a VCR, and his own phone. When I got sent to my room, there was nothing but a bed and a book, and a schoolbook at that. If I were a kid today, I'd *try* to get sent to my room.

My daddy believed in discipline. Floyd Leon never, ever told me, "Wait till you get home." My daddy believed that a child should be disciplined whenever and wherever he committed the sin. That's my daddy's heart.

Floyd Leon was a fast-pitch softball player. He was an old windmill-style pitcher, and he could really hum it in the Austin league. He was *good*. He was probably the third best pitcher, right behind Mr. Culp and Mr. Craig. They did big write-ups in the paper back then about fast-pitch softball, and my daddy was often featured in the paper.

Between innings, he would come off the field and up to the bleachers where my little mama was sitting. My mama didn't learn to drive until she was in her thirties, so she was pretty much a hostage there at the ballpark.

Daddy would ask Mama, "Everything goin' all right, baby love?"

She'd usually say, "Well, I'm fine, but I don't know where Dennis is. I have no idea where *your son* is."

About that time, I would run up from the back of the bleachers and say, "Hi, Daddy."

Floyd would poke his finger in my chest and say, "Do you know what the score is, boy?"

Still catching my breath from running up the bleachers, I would pant, "7–2?"

"Wrong." He'd grab hold of me and *whomp, whomp*—"Sit down!"—*whomp*. "Do you want some popcorn?"

Daddy was the kind of man who could discipline you and

then immediately fellowship with you. At the softball games, he would discipline me and then give me popcorn. It was over. That was my daddy—pure and simple.

FOOD FOR THOUGHT

Whom the LORD loves He chastens.

—Hebrews 12:6

When God wanted us to understand him in human terms, he called himself Father. Jesus called God *"Abba,"* which is the familiar Aramaic word for "Daddy," a warm term of endearment that speaks of God's love and care.

The author of the Book of Hebrews spoke of God's discipline: "My son, do not regard lightly the discipline of the LORD, nor faint when you are reproved by Him; for those whom the LORD loves He disciplines, and He scourges every son whom He receives" (12:5–6 NASB).

God does discipline his children. How, when, and where he chooses to discipline us belong to his own unknowable power and wisdom. Sometimes God disciplines us by taking something away. At other times he disciplines us by letting us have exactly what we think we want; only later do we discover that it was not his best for us.

As we seek to become disciples of Jesus Christ, we should never forget that the word *disciple* is directly related to the word *discipline*. To be a disciple of the Lord Jesus Christ is to know his discipline.

Yet just like Floyd Leon, God does not remain angry after he disciplines his children. One of the great promises of God's Word is found in Isaiah 57:16: "I will not contend forever, nor will I always be angry; for the spirit would fail before Me, and the souls which I have made."

God does not discipline in anger, nor does he stay angry. His discipline is not like human wrath. He knows that mere weak, mortal people could not stand the blast of his divine anger. God always disciplines out of love, not out of wrath.

Nineteenth-century lyricist Frederick W. Faber, whose work includes "Faith of Our Fathers," penned the words of "There's a Wideness in God's Mercy," which beautifully speaks of God's mercy in the midst of his justice.

> There's a wideness in God's mercy like the
> wideness of the sea;
> There's a kindness in His justice which is more
> than liberty.
> There is welcome for the sinner and more graces
> for the good;
> There is mercy with the Savior; there is healing
> in His blood.

Faber caught just the right note when he wrote, "There's a kindness in His justice." When God disciplines us, he only does it so that we might be renewed in fellowship with him—just like Daddy wanted to fellowship right after he whomped me.

I miss those softball nights, but I cherish the lessons. Thanks, Dad, for the memories!

When I misbehaved in
church, I'd get a hard
thump from Floyd Leon.
He'd look at the preacher
and mouth the words,
"I'll handle the boy."

Chapter 6

THUMPIN'
AND
PINCHIN'

God is smart. He made families the way they are because he knows we need mamas and daddies. They balance one another out on the scales of life. God's creation is full of forces that balance one another. For example, the chemical formula for regular table salt is NaCl. Those are the chemical symbols for sodium and chlorine. Each of those elements by itself can be volatile and flammable. But when you put the two of them together, you have table salt.

Or consider a great aircraft carrier. If you chunked any one piece of that huge, metal vessel into the ocean, that piece would sink. But when you put all the pieces together, the thing floats.

In a way, parents are like that. Daddy is the brick, and mama is the velvet. Daddy is the prosecuting attorney, and mama is the counsel for the defense. Children run to daddy when the monster in the closet is after them, and they run to mama when they are hurt.

You remember that Floyd Leon could whomp me on the head and then want to fellowship? Mama never could do that. Mama would hold a grudge for two or three days. After I committed some misdemeanor, it would be awhile before she got over it.

Sitting at the supper table, Mama would look at me and say, "Do you feel bad about it now?"

I couldn't even remember what sin I had committed! But I tried to look very remorseful.

She would say, "I hope you feel bad about it. Do you feel bad? Come here. Come to Mother. Tell me right here. Tell me right now."

I would put on a very solemn face. "Mama, I feel bad."

"All right. Hug your mother; everything's fine."

My daddy was a disciplinarian. When I misbehaved in church, I'd get a hard thump from Floyd Leon. My daddy was raised as a sharecropper, and he could pick that cotton. He had big, tough hands.

He'd look at the preacher and mouth the words, "I'll handle the boy." Boom!

I had my first vision when my daddy thumped me in

church. I had a vision of Jim and Tammy Faye coming down a waterslide.

He thumped me a second time, and I saw the Crystal Cathedral in California before Robert Schuller ever designed it.

He thumped me a third time, and I saw a six-hundred-foot Jesus in Oklahoma long before Oral Roberts ever did.

I'm just sharing my testimony: no drugs, no alcohol, just visions.

On the other hand, my mother would reach over and grab me by the hangy-down part of my arm. She would pinch and twist, right there in church.

I'd jerk a little at the pinch, and then Floyd would thump me. Boom! I call that child abuse in the church.

My little mama sure knew how to pinch and twist. She did that to me all through high school, even when I was a football player with an athletic build and a cocky strut.

She would say, "I don't care if you're state champ this, state champ that, you are going to mind your mother. Do you hear me?"

Then she'd sneak up behind me, grab hold of my arm, and just pinch and twist. "Come with Mama." She could take me anywhere.

The next day, walking down the hallway at school, some of my buddies said, "Hey, Swan, you got a hickie on the back of your arm. Who gave it to you?"

And I had to say, "My mother." How humiliating that my first hickie came from my mama.

⟜ Chapter Six ⟝

FOOD FOR THOUGHT

Children, obey your parents in the Lord, for this is right.

—Ephesians 6:1

One of the fascinating studies in the Gospels is how Jesus related to his parents. When Jesus, at twelve years of age, stayed behind in the temple at Passover, Joseph and Mary frantically looked for him (see Luke 2:45–51). After they finally found their son, they complained about their anxiety while looking for him.

The twelve-year-old Jesus showed remarkable balance in his response to his parents. On the one hand, he let them know respectfully but clearly that his first allegiance was to God. Yet when he returned to his home in Nazareth, he "was subject to them" (v. 51). That means that he arranged his life under their leadership and submitted himself to their care.

Certainly Jesus learned manly life from his earthly father, Joseph, as an apprentice in his carpenter shop. The great artist Georges de La Tour created beautiful paintings of Jesus in the carpenter shop with Joseph. In one of these paintings, Jesus holds a light while Joseph works with wood. The light just barely illuminates a cross-shaped piece of wood on the floor in the corner of the picture, foreshadowing the death Jesus knew he would face.

Most Christians believe that Joseph was quite a bit older than Mary and left her a widow before Jesus departed from home. As a grown man entering his ministry, Jesus redefined his relationship with his mother in terms of God's will for his life (see Mark 3:31–35).

One time, Jesus' mother seemed to want Jesus to show his hand as Messiah before the appointed time. Jesus gently reminded her that the wedding at Cana was not the right time for his announcement (see John 2:4). While Jesus was dying on the cross, he took time to instruct the disciple John to take care of his widowed mother (see John 19:26–27).

At all times Jesus' relationship with his parents was what it should be. When Jesus was young, he was subject to them. When he was a mature man, he reminded his mother that God's will came first in his life. When he was dying, he took care of his mother's earthly and heavenly future. As always, Jesus is our model for life.

We need to turn to Jesus Christ for wisdom as we relate to our parents, even when they thump us or pinch us. Come to think of it, we could all probably use a little more thumpin' and pinchin' from our heavenly Father! Remember, he disciplines those whom he loves.

We kids qualified Mama's Toni by how many mud daubers were affected when Grandma dabbed on that stinky, milky, murky liquid.

THE TONI

Do you remember Sucrets? Not many of us ever took one of those elusive throat lozenges, but we can sure remember things that were stored in the boxes long after the lozenges were gone. A Sucrets box was a multifaceted thing. Our family had one that was mainly used to store bobby pins; it only came forth at a special time in our life—when Mama got a Toni!

Mama periodically saved up to buy a Toni home-permanent kit. She got so excited when she purchased one at the supermarket. She was pumped! It was a monumental moment for Mama.

Her getting a Toni was likened in the Swanberg family to her being the winner on the fifties television show *Queen for a*

Day. It was Mama's new lease on life. It was her moment in the sun and our moment of nasal dismay. That stuff stank!

It was an event that was precipitated by many phone calls to aunts, grandparents, sisters, and friends. It was almost newsworthy in the local *Grit* magazine. And it was the catalyst for Mama's disposition for the next couple of months.

We would pray, "Lord Jesus, give us a good Toni for the family's sake. If Mama's not happy, nobody's happy."

On some Toni adventures, we traveled to Grandpa and Grandma Johnson's house in the country. Grandma Bell would administer the Toni on the front porch, next to the old church bench. All of the Toni paraphernalia would be laid on the church bench, but not to rest.

We kids usually sat out in the cotton field on a terrace and watched. This was a sight that I must explain.

Grandma always began by washing Mama's hair in a big white porcelain pan with a red rim, the one we kids were bathed in when we were babies. After slinging Mama's hair back, Grandma twisted it to wring it out. Then out came the comb. Grandma pulled it through Mama's hair, taking out the tangles. We watched Mama wince, but she was willing to endure the pain for the excitement of getting a Toni.

Grandma started with a strand of hair, poured on the milky solution, and then put a square of toilet tissue on Mama's hair. Next she rolled that strand of hair around a pencil and slid the curl down to Mama's head. With two bobby pins from the Sucrets box, she pinned Mama's new Toni curl down!

The Toni

We were waiting for the Toni bottle; that stuff stank to high heaven. It was not a sweet aroma to the Lord. But Grandma seemed to enjoy the smell. When she took that bottle and poured it on Mama's hair, the ozone layer visibly changed. We cringed, Mama held her nose, and Grandma inhaled. Even the mud daubers took off from their nest under the eaves of the porch!

We loved watching those mud daubers get out of the way. Their formation was, *Everyone on your own; abandon mission.* They weren't the Blue Angels, but they were the Flying Daubers, reminiscent of the Flying Tigers of World War II!

We kids qualified Mama's Toni's by how many mud daubers were affected when Grandma dabbed on that stinky, milky, murky liquid.

That day on Grandma's porch, Mama's Toni was a nine-dauber 'do. Others ranged between four and seven, but that day was the one and only nine-dauber 'do.

Those were the days. Life's joys were there for all of us: Mama, Grandma, we kids, and the mud daubers.

We enjoyed the elementary things of life. Looking back, I realize that those times were memorable and noteworthy. They were our basic education before entering the upper-level courses of life.

Mama was satisfied with a Toni, whereas moms today want a nine-dauber special at a nine-chair salon. Who knows how they do hair today? It's all done behind closed doors. In those days, it was done on the porch. We were family, and we all experienced it together.

Mama even went to the grocery store with her hair in pins to show off her impending moment of glory. Her hair would soon unfold and hold. We would be blessed, and Mama would be transformed.

Now when I open my medicine cabinet and see a Sucrets box, I remember those Toni moments and am reminded of how good life was, is, and will be. Every family needs a box of memories.

FOOD FOR THOUGHT

Hope does not disappoint.
—Romans 5:5

He that hath an ear, let me make this clear. Life is like a Sucrets box. It is filled with things that hold our lives together...simple things like bobby pins and, most of all, memories.

It's important that families have memories around boxes that have real substance. A Dutch family had a memorable box. During the awful dark days of World War II, the family had very little food. Every day the older kids had to scour the streets just to find enough to keep body and soul together. The little children often expressed their fears about the future.

The widowed mother had a clever way to calm their fears. She would point to a box high up on the kitchen shelf. It was a metal box with a lid, like an old cracker box. As she pointed, she would say, "If worse comes to worst, we can always open the box."

For years, the children wondered what the box held. They speculated that it contained money, expensive jewelry, or some other kind of treasure. They thought that it might hide some kind of magic food that would last a long time. Yet none of them ever dared to look into the box.

Many years passed, and the mother finally passed on to glory. As her adult children gathered in the empty house before the memorial service, they all wondered the same thing. *What's in the box?*

Finally the oldest son reached high up on the shelf and took the box down. It was old, rusted, and covered with dust. He gently pried the lid off as the others watched intently. They all peered into the box to see.

To their astonishment, the box was empty. Their hope for all these years had been an empty box.

As Christians, we know that our hope is not an empty box. As the apostle Paul wrote, "We rejoice in the hope of the glory of God. And hope does not disappoint" (Romans 5:2, 5 NIV). Our hope is genuine because it is tied to the triumph of the Lord Jesus Christ. Hope is substantial. Hope is concrete. Hope is real.

For Christians, hope is not an empty box; it's even more than a Sucrets box full of memories. It's a box full of possibilities because of our Lord Jesus Christ, who is our Blessed Hope, Redeemer, and Friend.

Those two cubes went choo, choo across the room. My daddy discovered the Heimlich maneuver right then and there.

Chapter 8

JELL-O CUBES

These days it seems we are faced with the difficulty of "overchoice"; we have so many options we don't know what to choose. Folks can have two hundred television channels and not be able to find a thing to watch. We used to think it was great to have one or two channels. Remember when you could go to the magazine stand and the whole thing only had about twenty magazines? Now there are thousands of them. One of the few times we had a variety of choices when I was growing up was when we went to the cafeteria. My daddy and my mama *love* going to cafeterias.

Just the other day, my daddy called me long-distance and said, "Hey, Den, uh, have you heard the good news?"

"What's that, Dad?"

"At Luby's, they've got the Luann Plus Platter now."

"The Luann Plus Platter?"

"Yeah, it's only for a month. You get the half portions. You get salad, your tea, and your dessert all for the price of one."

"Okay, Dad."

The next thing I knew, I had my family at the local cafeteria. My wife is always telling me, "You're getting more Floydish all the time." I can't help it. It's just sort of in my blood.

I can still recall the things my daddy would say at the cafeteria. I remember the trays and the silverware. Daddy called it "hardware."

"Everybody get your hardware. Get your hardware now," he'd command.

If you didn't get your hardware and got to the table without it, uh-oh. That upset him. Then he'd have to get the tea lady.

"Uh, tea lady! Tea lady, right here—we need some hardware!"

We'd be embarrassed and say, "Shhhhh, Dad."

Dad's second priority was, "Everybody drink water. Good night, I'm not paying what they charge for tea. If you want tea, drink tea at home. *Everybody drink water.*"

I remember the people in front of us putting their tea back. It's amazing how people listen to Floyd Leon.

Then my daddy would add, "And everybody leave the desserts alone. Good night, we don't need any desserts. We've got melorine ice cream at home."

Jell-O Cubes

I don't know if you've ever had melorine, but it was *not* ice cream. It was not like what we have in Texas called Blue Bell. It was not creamy. It was not even ice milk. It was some kind of vegetable shortening concocted to look like the real thing! But if you left a bowl of melorine out on the snack bar, it just sort of foamed up into a little wad. We'd get it in Neapolitan flavor. We kids would eat the chocolate and vanilla and leave the strawberry for Floyd Leon. The strawberry portion reminded me of whipped-up Pepto Bismol. And it had about the same effect!

Nevertheless, Daddy would eat it and say, "Isn't this good?"

Friends, it was nothing but foam.

Once at the cafeteria, I was going through the line and saw a bowl of Jell-O cubes. I wanted that Jell-O so badly. The cubes were so colorful…so inviting.

I asked, "Daddy, could I have some Jell-O cubes?"

He said, "Good night, Den, you don't eat Jell-O unless you've got a twenty-four-hour bug."

Come to think of it, I don't think we ever did eat Jell-O unless we were sick. Jell-O is like creamed chicken on toast or chicken-noodle soup—comfort food. But I really wanted that Jell-O.

My mother heard Dad's comment and decided that she'd had enough. When moms have had enough, they have had enough. She looked at my daddy and said, "That's enough,

Floyd Leon. You are too hard on him, and I'm tired of it. We're all tired of it." Right there in public.

As soon as my mother turned her head, my dad looked at me and growled, "You better eat every cube of it!"

I got the Jell-O on my tray. I don't know why, but I sucked a couple of cubes out of the bowl. I thought it was funny.

Daddy didn't think it was funny. *Whomp! Whomp!* Those two cubes went *choo, choo* across the room. My daddy discovered the Heimlich maneuver right then and there.

But this is the bad part: There was a man behind us I'd never seen before. He was the kind of man who had a big tummy, a western belt, and nothing but a prayer holding up his Levi's.

He chuckled and said to my dad, "Good hit! Good hit!"

My dad looked at this man as if they'd been old high-school buddies and nodded, "It don't hurt 'em. It *don't hurt* 'em."

The man agreed. "He'll thank you for it someday."

I have yet to thank my daddy for that one!

FOOD FOR THOUGHT

Do not love the world or the things in the world.
—1 John 2:15

Life is pretty much like a cafeteria line—it offers us many choices, both good and bad. When he was an old man, the beloved disciple John wrote a warning about the world: "Love not the world, neither the things that are in the world....For all that is in the world, the lust of the flesh, and the lust of the eyes, and the pride of life, is not of the Father, but is of the world. And the world passeth away, and the lust thereof: but he that doeth the will of God abideth for ever" (1 John 2:15–17 KJV).

Some people live to be cool, hip, and in the know. Some are drawn to the spectacles that appeal to the eyes. Others become proud about their ability to sustain their own. John says that these kinds of "delicacies" will pass away with the world.

This world is passing before our eyes like a parade that will come to an end. The only thing that will last is the Word of God. How can we be sure that we are not carried away by the many choices of life? Paul gives sound advice in Philippians 1:10: "Approve the things that are excellent."

The Christian must have a spiritual radar that detects the difference not only between bad and good but also among good, better, and best. Have you ever spent time in the clean air of the desert or the ocean? After you've done that, your nose is more sensitive when you return to the odors and smells of the city. The purity of the clean air refines your sense of smell so that every fragrance is more detectable.

The Lord Jesus wants us to spend enough time with him in the Word and in prayer that we are sensitive to the good and bad choices in the cafeteria line of life. He wants us to make our choices in this life with real discernment. At the highest levels of the normal Christian life, we should be able to detect the faintest difference in things that please and displease our

Lord. Like a husband and wife who have lived together for fifty years and know immediately without saying or looking what the other thinks, so we should grow in intimacy in our relationship with our Lord Jesus. Let's go through the cafeteria line of life with him as the only Server and with the constant attitude, "Lord, put on my plate only what you want me to have."

And let him be the one to say, "There's always room for Jell-O."

Vacations are times for
being with the people you
love, letting your hair
down, relaxing, and making
lifelong memories.

Chapter

SWANBERG VACATIONS

In the fast pace of American life, we often lose sight of our need for time away, for days out of the rut of the routine. The ancients had a saying: "The bowstring that is always stretched will finally lose its strength." In their day, bows were strung with animal hide. It was necessary to detach the hide string from one end of the bow when it was not in use. If you did not, the string would overstretch and lose its tautness. Then it could no longer shoot an arrow.

The intervals of difference—of occasionally loosening the bowstring—give meaning. Let's consider other examples. Music is written with notes and rests. Without silences between the notes, the music would make no sense. Your very heart beats and then pauses for a moment. The tides of the seas ebb and flow every twelve hours. Seasons change. The moon waxes and wanes. Geese fly south and then north. Bears hunt, eat, and then hibernate. Salmon swim downstream and thousands of miles out into the ocean, where they rest and eat until their arduous swim back upstream to spawn.

Why do some humans consider themselves exceptions from this rhythm? We need the wisdom to know that we all need time to get away. I remember vividly the significance of our family vacations, even though they were simple and modest times.

The Swanberg clan loved taking vacations. They were limited because my daddy served in the Thirty-Sixth Infantry Division of the National Guard in Austin, Texas. His two weeks of vacation were always used up playing army at Fort Hood. Therefore, when we took a vacation, it was over a weekend.

Since we lived by Austin, we weren't far from Galveston, Texas. Going to Galveston was a big-time vacation for us. We'd load up our car and hook 'em to the beach. We always packed an Igloo ice chest and rolled all the windows down. As we had no air conditioning, we angled the vents on the front windows to pick up a good breeze. My sisters and I hoped those vents wouldn't suck in too many bugs; they always seemed to whomp us upside the head. We sipped happily on Big Orange as we drove on down the highway.

My older sister, Sherry Darlene, my little sister, Teri Linn, and the Swan rode in the backseat while Floyd Leon and Pauline Bernadeen manned the front. From time to time we would alternate, and one of us would get to sit up front between Mama and Daddy. It seemed like the best place to sit. We usually drove until we came to a roadside park then dug into the ice chest full of sandwiches, potato salad, and all the trimmings. To this day, I think food tastes best when you eat it outside.

We never stopped to eat at a restaurant on the way. We were thrifty Swedes; we believed in saving money. At least my daddy always did. I guess that's why my parents still have something these days. They were conscientious and good stewards. And we passed right on by many Stuckey's souvenir shops.

We kids would ask Daddy over and over, "Come on, Daddy, let's stop at Stuckey's."

He would say, "We're making good time, but we have to keep going. We don't have time for Stuckey's. We can do that some other time."

We hardly ever got to stop at Stuckey's. But every now and then, Daddy would stop. What a joy it was to go into Stuckey's, the world's greatest souvenir shop. There were all kinds of treasures in there: cartooned toilet, a Texas sized cigar, a corncob pipe, and a toy outhouse that, when you opened up the front door, the little fellow turned around and, you know, on you. One time we purchased a "poop" cushion without Mama and Daddy seeing us. What a gift. To us, that was the best treasure of all. We paid for it and got back in the car.

We were driving down the road, and I blew up the "poop" cushion. Then I sat on it and giggled. Daddy said, "Good night. Y'all stop that."

We had so much fun with that "poop" cushion. But finally it had a blowout, and there went the joy.

In Galveston we stayed at a place called the S.S. Snort. It was small and had a little kitchen that connected to a room that we shared with another family. Our room had two beds: Mama and Daddy slept in one bed; Darlene and Teri shared the other. I slept on an air mattress on the floor. Usually we got there so late that we went straight to bed.

The next morning we'd pump up the inner tubes from Grandpa's tractor and head for the Gulf waves. We had the time of our lives.

The thing that made those Swanberg vacations so much fun was the fact that we were together. And when we did things together, we had fun together. Our priority was our relationships with one another and the fellowship that took place because of those special relationships. That's what vacations are all about. Vacations are times for being with the people you love, letting your hair down, relaxing, and making lifelong memories.

FOOD FOR THOUGHT

Come aside by yourselves to a deserted place and rest a while.
—Mark 6:31

God did a lot with those men and women who were willing to take time and go apart with him. Moses spent forty days on top of Mount Sinai in a retreat with God. Out of that quietness and silence, God gave humanity the Ten Commandments and a whole new way of life. Elijah the prophet went aside with God to the area of Mount Horeb and heard God speak in a still, small voice. The Lord Jesus spent forty days in the desert, wrestling with his own destiny as the Son of God. He left that period filled with the Holy Spirit and charged with energy for his public ministry. After his experience with the risen Christ on the Damascus road, the apostle Paul spent three years in the Syrian desert, listening to God and preparing to evangelize the world. He left that period of retreat to become the mightiest missionary in history.

We need to plunge into the depth of recreating retreats and revitalizing vacations. Such times must not just be filled with frantic agendas to visit every tourist destination. They should be times of true renewal—a slower pace, a conversation with God, and a temporary cessation of the daily grind.

Perhaps you might find yourself on an "enforced vacation," a time of silence or stillness through no planning of your own. The loss of a job, an illness, or some other tragic circumstance may cross your path and slow you down. If this has happened to you, don't be discouraged. God has mightily used such enforced vacations in the lives of his people. Martin Luther translated the Bible while forced to hide in a German castle. John Bunyan wrote *Pilgrim's Progress* while in prison in Bedford, England. Dietrich Bonhoeffer wrote monumental Christian literature from a concentration camp. These are just a few examples of what God can do when we take time with him.

Why not get away to see what God would do with you? You'll be glad you did!

My daddy looked me squarely in the eyes and repeated his command, "Hug your mother!"

Chapter 10

HUG
YOUR
MOTHER

Hugs are definitely healing. Psychologists have measured the effects of hugging and documented that folks who get hugged have lower blood pressure, fewer serious diseases, less depression, and a greater sense of well-being than those who don't get hugged (as long as you discount Mike Tyson's hug of Evander Hollyfield just before the bite that ended the fight).

I remember well my high-school days. My little mama, Pauline Bernadeen, bless her heart, would get so upset with me so often. I'd put on my old jeans, boots, and a football jersey and try to walk out of the house in those clothes. You know how kids go through that stage. I just looked horrible.

Mama would say, "Dennis, you look awful. Your father and

I work so hard for you kids. It hurts. It hurts. I wouldn't be caught dead wearing that."

"Mama, what do you mean?"

"I wonder what your teachers think of your mother?"

"Well, Mama, you don't go to school up there."

"You are a reflection of your mother."

"Lord, help me."

Oh my poor little mama. What I put her through back then.

I remember when I began to like the high-school girls. I'd try my best to wow them by using different voices to entertain them. They thought I was a nut and a clown, but I got their attention. You know, you'll almost do anything for attention when you have attention deficit disorder. You sort of become the class clown. Your focus is here, there, and yonder. That was the old Swan.

I'd gather a crowd and next thing I knew, I'd be trying to impress a girl with a poem I learned from my high-school football chaplain, Marshall "Rabbi" Edwards. Once I had my crowd, I'd quote:

> When angels fashioned thee, my love,
> They took the very fairest things to make you
>   fair;
> Took two perfect seashells for your ears,
> And robbed the morning sunbeams for your
>   hair.
> From the sky came the stars which art your eyes

The rose was robbed to paint your sweet mouth
   red,
And then the angels smiled and from a bird
   they took the brain
And placed it in your lovely head.

I played football in high school. I was one of those typical high-school athletes. We'd finish football practice, and the coach would say, "All right, take it on in, boys." I'd hear that and, man, I'd take off. I loved to sing country music, so I'd take my helmet off and sing into it. I loved the echo it made. I'd head off the field singing like old Hank Williams, "Your cheatin' heart will make you weep. Yee-ha."

The coach would say, "Someone pull a groin?"

"No, that's old Swanberg singing."

"Good. I thought someone hurt himself."

I'd go back to the locker room, get cleaned up, and head home. Little Pauline Bernadeen was always waiting for me.

I love my mama. She's the kind that loves to clean ears, you know what I mean? Many times she'd have her Sucrets box full of bobby pins opened up. She would take one out and say, "Your ears are filthy; let me at them."

I'd protest, but I was trained to endure the pain for the Lord, so I stood still as she dug in there. My mama could really clean ears. But the main thing she wanted was a hug. After the ritual ear cleaning, she'd say, "Now hug your mother."

I'd say, "Aw, Mama, I don't want to hug ya."

"I said, hug your mother."

"Mama, I ain't gonna hug on ya." (You know how you go through that stage.)

I knew Mama was upset when she doubled-up on syllables and her shoulders shook. She'd say, "So-on, I said, hu-ug your mo-o-ther." Boy, I didn't like it when she cried.

I'd try to comfort her. "Oh, Mama."

"I remember when you were a little boy and you used to hug your mother all the time," she'd sob.

"Mama, that makes up for now, then."

"No, it doesn't. I want them always. I always want those hugs."

"Oh, Mama."

One time, Floyd Leon, sitting back over yonder in a Lazy Boy recliner, suddenly paid attention. Dads hear what they want to hear. He knew that if Mama was unhappy, later on he'd be unhappy.

So he grabbed that lever on the side of the recliner and raised his six-feet-two-inch and two-hundred-and-twenty-pound frame. He thundered, "Boy, you better hug your mother right now."

I didn't argue with Floyd Leon. I put my arms around Mama—barely.

She protested, "That is not a hug."

I looked at my daddy. He looked me squarely in the eyes and repeated his command, "Hug your mother!"

Man, I picked Mama up. I squeezed her tight. I kissed her right on the lips, like in the movies.

When I put her down, she wiped her mouth with the back of her sleeve. "Phew! I'm your mother!"

I said, "Well, I hugged you, Mama."

"I don't care for that kind of huggin' and kissin' on my mouth."

"Well, isn't that the way you and Daddy kiss?"

"No, it isn't."

You know what I said? "Poor old Daddy!"

Those were the days. The early years are so important and should be full of fun. If you've got little kids or little grandkids, enjoy them. Their earliest years are the best times in life. We look back and laugh on those days, don't we?

I've got two boys. Lord have mercy. My mother used to tell me, "When you grow up and get married, I hope you have two boys just like you." Well, God got me, and I'm paying for my childhood. My littlest one, Dusty, is just like his daddy—he also has attention deficit disorder. Sometimes he and I get together just to release all of our energy. We wrestle! We have the Swan's Wrestling Federation Main Event whenever I return home from the road. Dusty's the Macho Man and I'm the American Dream Dusty Rhodes! We bond together, and we have a good time.

Let me tell you, life is meant to be enjoyed, and it is always more enjoyable when you have good, healthy relationships. When you have a healthy relationship with your family and friends, you're more likely to laugh and not take yourself too seriously. We're all on a journey. We're all growing. We're all striving to be where we need to be. I want to encourage you to lighten up and enjoy your life. Laugh a little bit; it won't hurt you. It might just set you free and keep you going. My sons, Chad and Dusty, remind me of this truth every day!

FOOD FOR THOUGHT

For as he thinks in his heart, so is he.

—Proverbs 23:7

The new pioneers of alternative medicine emphasize the incredible significance that our mental attitude plays in our physical health. People are just as old, just as sick, just as young, just as energetic as they think they are. The writer of Proverbs got it right when he said, "As [a man] thinketh in his heart, so is he" (23:7 KJV). It's funny that modern medicine is just catching up with the Word of God.

In *Care of the Soul,* psychiatrist Thomas Moore points out the incredible significance of mothers and fathers in our lives. Taking care of the soul means, among other things, being solidly part of daily life in the midst of a family. According to Dr. Moore, ear cleanings and hugging sessions help to create a healthy soul. Families need legends, stories, myths, and episodes to pass from one generation to the next. Such stories give children roots and a context.

Ear cleanings and hugs don't seem like much at the time. But in reality, they are the stuff that builds families and lives.

Part Two

LIV ING

OUT THE CALL

They dunked me underneath
the water and wouldn't let
me up until I said "tithe."

TILL THEY BUBBLE

Baptists get their name from baptizing people. There's something a little funny, when you think of it, about ceremoniously dunking people under water at a public gathering. At elementary-school carnivals kids find it hilarious to throw a softball, hit that little metal paddle, and send their principal into a tank of water. But Baptists do it with great solemnity as an ordinance of the church. Actually, the Greek word *baptizo* means to dunk somebody under the water. I found out personally what *baptizo* meant while I was away at college.

I'd always wanted to go to a state college and party, party, party—you know, build a testimony (just kidding). But where did I go? I went to a church school—Baylor University (also known as "Jerusalem on the Brazos"). Since I was a Methodist,

🫑 *Chapter Eleven* 🫑

I was nervous about attending a Baptist school in the heart of Texas (Waco, Texas, to be exact—the home of Dr. Pepper, the "Baptist brew"!). I thought it would be like a monastery or something. But when I got there, I discovered that the students weren't "holier-than-thou" at all. They were regular people—sinners just like everybody else.

Now, the students at Baylor didn't dance much. When they did, they had to do it off campus, and they had to call it a "function." Some of those students could really "function" with an "unction." And those girls could smooch! They knew how to greet you with a "holy kiss." I decided that I'd rather smooch than dance any day and soon knew it was time to cross over to Baptist life!

So one Sunday I walked the aisle at Columbus Avenue Baptist Church and took the pastor's extended hand.

"Yes, what's your decision?" he asked.

I was just a regular old dude then. I hadn't been "called" yet. So I said, "I want to join up."

"Well, have you been saved?"

"March 15, 1971, on a Monday night at 8:00."

"Good, good." He nodded his head. "Have you been baptized?"

I grinned. "A little dab'll do ya."

He frowned. "A little dab won't do you here."

"Well, what do y'all do?" I was confused.

"We put you under till you bubble."

The next thing I knew, I was in the baptismal room—the architect's afterthought consisting of whatever is left over next to the heating and air-conditioning units. There's all kinds of junk in these rooms: an old bale of hay from the last Christmas cantata, last year's "Together We Build" sign with the Hallelujah Goal fallen off, old boxes of minutes from committee meetings in years gone by—all kinds of stuff.

I had only seen one other person immersed, and that had been a long time ago. So there I was, standing in the baptismal room, and I didn't know what to do. I was about to encounter my first Baptist deacon—you know, the kind of guy with a big tummy and a short tie. Well, this deacon came into the baptismal room to check up on me, and he just sort of stood there, looking at me. So I finally asked him, "Man, what do I do?"

He said, "Rub up."

"What?"

"Rub up."

"What?"

"Rub up!" Then he grunted and pointed to some culottes outfits hanging on a rack.

The lightbulb came on. I asked, "Robe up?"

He let out an exasperated sigh. "I said rub up three times."

But I wasn't about to put on one of those sissy outfits. "Man, I'm an athlete here at Baylor University. I ain't gonna put on some culottes."

He looked at me sternly and said, "Ye are if ye love the Lord."

"Where does it say that in the Bible?"

"Hezekiah 4."

Now don't look too long for that one. It ain't in there. But it worked for that old deacon. The next thing I knew, I was wearing a culottes outfit, and that deacon had slapped a piece of tape on my left shoulder with my name on it. (You know, it's bad when the pastor gets into the baptismal pool and forgets the name of the person he's baptizing. He can't turn to the audience and say, "Let's all say this brother's name together." And it doesn't go well to say, "This is, uh, Bubba.") So the deacon put that piece of tape on my shoulder with an *M* underneath my name. The *M* stood for "Methodist," meaning, "This one stays under just a little longer." Then they dunked me underneath the water and wouldn't let me up until I said "tithe."

FOOD FOR THOUGHT

As many of us as were baptized into Christ Jesus
were baptized into His death.

—Romans 6:3

Baptism is a wonderful way to give your Christian testimony. There are other ways to let your friends and neighbors know about your new faith—you could rent one of those old sound trucks and go around town making an announcement on a loud speaker: "I am Joe Dokes, and I am now a Christian."

Or you could rent a bulletin board, put your picture on it, and write a caption: "Joe Dokes, pictured here, is a Christian."

Or if you're rich, you could buy a moment during the Super Bowl: "Let us introduce you to Joe Dokes, a Christian who is a champion."

But God had something different in mind. Baptism witnesses to all that we are believers in the Lord Jesus Christ.

Even Jesus was baptized to show that he identified with us. He went down to the Jordan River and stood in line with a bunch of sinners, waiting for his cousin John to baptize him (see Matthew 3:13–17). He stood where he really did not belong. There was likely a harlot in front of him and a hardened tax collector behind him. But in order to identify with us all, he stood in line.

One of the most famous books of the fifties was *Black Like Me*. It was the story of John H. Griffin, a student at Texas Christian University who dyed his skin black and went to live in the old South to write about what it was like to be black. He was able to write an amazing book about the struggles of black people because he identified with them. He literally walked in their shoes to experience their lives.

The baptism of the Lord Jesus was like that. He identified with us by standing in a line he did not need to stand in. He set the example.

When we are baptized, we identify with Jesus Christ through his death, burial, and resurrection. First, we are to so identify with the Lord Jesus Christ that we *die* with him. A dead person cannot commit sin. Because of our new identity with Jesus, we are to consider ourselves dead to sin. Then, when we go down into that water, we are *buried* with Jesus. But that's not all. Just as the Lord Jesus Christ came up out of the tomb, we, too, are *raised* to new life when we come up out of the water. We are now alive to God in Christ Jesus. What a great Savior!

By being submerged beneath the water and then coming up out of the water, we confess a total identification with the Lord Jesus Christ. There is just something about being drenched from the top of your head to the soles of your feet that totally confesses the Lord Jesus Christ.

Baptism may be the first sermon a new believer preaches. Just as a married person puts on a ring or a soldier puts on a uniform, a Christian seals his or her testimony with baptism.

The old spiritual asks,

> Were you there when they crucified my Lord?
> Were you there when they laid him in the tomb?
> Were you there when he rose up from the dead?

The baptized person answers, "Yes, I was there. I identified with his death, burial, and resurrection."

Paul writes about this in a striking passage from Romans: "Do you not know that as many of us as were baptized into Christ Jesus were baptized into His death? Therefore we were buried with Him through baptism into death, that just as Christ was raised from the dead by the glory of the Father, even so we also should walk in newness of life" (Romans 6:3–4). The Lord Jesus Christ left the glories of heaven and came down to earth for us. He identified with us in all of our needs so that we could identify with him in all of his glory.

And, when I think about it, Jesus' love is just bubbling over in me!

I broke into an impersonation of Billy Graham and said, "Won't you come? Others are coming. We have some coupons here, some li-ter-a-ture. These aisles are full of cans—I know you can. Won't you come?"

STRUCK BY "THE CALL"

Preachers come in all shapes and sizes. Some have outgoing personalities, and some are introverts. There are old and young preachers, famous and unknown, loud and soft, as well as a few rich and a lot of poor preachers. Some city preachers wear robes, and a lot of country parsons wear overalls.

One thing all preachers have in common, whether they or their congregations realize it, is that they are all human beings. They are saved and called humans, but they are humans.

The apostle Paul found that out when he suddenly got into a big mess. He was preaching in Asia Minor when a crowd of Lycaonian people cried out, "The gods have come down to us in the likeness of men" (Acts 14:11). They thought Paul was the Greek god Hermes because he did most of the talking, and

Chapter Twelve

they called Barnabas Zeus. Paul told those confused Greeks the most important thing preachers must realize about themselves: "We also are men with the same nature as you" (v. 15). You see, preachers can't really help human beings unless they are human beings. That's what I found out when "the call" fell on me.

I am a preacher, so I know preachers can be a bit peculiar. At one time in our lives, believe it or not, we were normal, average human beings. I remember it well—those were the days. I was just a regular guy. I'd say things like, "Hey! What's goin' on? Yeah!" A regular *Homo sapien*, you know what I mean? Then, when the call of God comes on you, you're "called." And when you're "called," several things happen.

First, you just start to look more pastoral, sort of like you have the flu. Next, you develop a "holy bob." You just sort of "bob" a lot—your head looks like a cork on a fishing pole. Have you ever noticed how preachers just bob, bob, bob? And have you noticed preachers' voices? This voice transformation happens gradually. Your voice goes up high, then it goes down low, and you talk that way wherever you go. If you're really called, you know what I mean. (If you don't talk that way, maybe you ought to check your call.)

I remember my freshman year at Baylor University, I was just a regular dude. Boy I was average, and I had a good time. I'd meet girls on campus and say, "Hey, what's goin' on? Want to go to a movie? Want to go out and get a coke?" Wow! Was I ever normal.

76

But on July 4, 1973, God called me into the ministry, and things started to change. It was tough to get a date after that. I'd call girls up on the phone, just like I had before I got the call.

They would answer, "Hello?"

I'd say, "Friend, this is Brother Dennis. I'd like to know if you would like to go out and fellowship awhile to share our hearts and burdens together in the Lord."

Most girls were not exactly fired up about that. Dating was tough even through my seminary days. I went to Southwestern Baptist Theological Seminary, in Fort Worth, Texas (also called "Cowtown USA"). When I got there I was exceedingly pastoral. I never will forget, though, when my wife-to-be, Lauree Wilkes, walked through the door with a singing group one night. She was just a little singer, the kind who takes the microphone and almost eats the thing. While she was singin' her heart out, I was in the back goin', "Hubba, hubba, hubba."

I went up to her after the concert and tried to act like a layman. I said, "Uh, hey, how ya doin'? I'm Dennis Swanberg." I got her name and phone number, but as soon as I turned away, the call hit me, and I became pastoral again.

The next night, I called her up for the big date. I got her on the phone and was trying hard to be a normal human. I started off sort of regular and said, "Lauree?"

She said, "Yes?"

And all of a sudden, the call hit. I said, "This is Brother Dennis. I wanted to call and inquire at this time in our lives whether you'd like to go out together and just see what great things God could have in store."

I was thinking, *Oh there it goes; I blew it.* But Lauree's mother was standing nearby and said, "Go out with him, Lauree. He is a man of God." In other words, "Do this for Jesus." So Lauree decided to take me on as a "project for God" and agreed to go out with me. We ate at the Italian Inn on the west side of Fort Worth, and we sat in one of those romantic little booths. I worked so hard to just be regular. Meanwhile, she was trying to relate to me as a minister.

She said, "You know, when I was a little girl I sensed God calling me to home missions."

I responded, "Oh, really? Baby, I am your *home-mission project!*"

She believed me, and we tied the knot on May 19, 1979.

You can spot preachers anywhere. You can even spot us at football games. The laymen will yell, "Oh man, come on ref…" They share that unknown tongue; you know what I mean. On the other hand, the preachers yell things like, "Oh my soul, mercy, mercy."

You can also spot us in the relatively mundane places of life. The other day I was in a grocery store, going down aisle 7. Have you noticed, ladies, that we men will not ask anybody where the Rotel is? We will hunt it down like we're huntin' quail. We'll look down every aisle without even reading the signs that hang up there over the aisles.

The stockboy can come by and offer, "Can I help you, sir?"

But we respond, "I've got it, son."

It takes us forever and a day. Well, just as I was going down aisle 7, a woman was coming up aisle 7. She had a basket with the cutest kid in the seat. I don't know what came over me other than the call of God.

I broke into an impersonation of Billy Graham and said, "Won't you come? Won't *you* come? Others are coming. Won't *you* come? Your basket will wait for you. Won't you come? We have some coupons here, some li-ter-a-ture. These aisles are full of cans—I know you can. Won't you come?"

Then all of a sudden I sort of snapped out of it and thought, *Swanberg, you're in the grocery store.* Then I hooked 'em down to the next aisle. I was so embarrassed. I don't know what came over me. That pastoral personality just hit me, you know?

During my last year of seminary, I finally got the phone call I was dreaming of. It came from First Baptist Church of Rogers, in central Texas.

They said, "Brother Dennis, we've got your résumé and your Xerox picture, and you look good to us. Would you like to come and be our pastor? Would you like to pray about it?"

I said, "I don't need to pray about it. I'm comin'." Friend, when you only get one invitation, *go.*

Lauree and I got down there and had the best time. First Baptist Church of Rogers is the greatest church in central Texas. We loved our country town, right between Buckholts and Heidenheimer. I preached my heart out Sunday after Sunday. I gave it everything I had.

I remember times when I'd be back there with the choir gettin' ready to go into the service. I'd say, "Choir, are y'all ready to go?" We were family. We were close. I wanted to start the service by 11:00 A.M. because by 11:55, the deacons would line up at the back as if a riot were about to happen. At high noon, they'd all look at their watches and pull their index fingers across their throats in unison.

One thing I found out for sure at Rogers, Texas, was that preachers and congregations both win when they understand that preachers are just humans.

FOOD FOR THOUGHT

Christ Jesus came into the world to save sinners,
of whom I am chief.
—1 Timothy 1:15

Paul found that out gradually. When he started out, he claimed a big title: "Paul, an apostle (not from men nor through man . . .)" (Galations 1:1). A few years down the missionary road, an older Paul wrote, "I am the least of the apostles, not worthy to be called an apostle" (1 Corinthians 15:9). Many years later, when Paul was on trial for his life, he had still another opinion of himself: "Christ Jesus came into the world to save sinners, of whom I am chief" (1 Timothy 1:15). Old Paul's opinion of his own humanity changed across thirty years.

Sometimes preachers pray, "Hide me behind the cross." Actually, there is no place to hide when you are a preacher, not even behind the cross. And the last thing we preachers need to do is to hide our humanity. We are simply starving people telling other starving people how to get the Bread of Life.

People love it when something goes wrong in church. Some were even saying, "Man, we ought to come here every Sunday."

Chapter 13

EASTER
SUNDAY
SURPRISE

For a preacher, Easter Sunday is big. It's what the Super Bowl is to a football player, the U.S. Open to a golfer, or the Indy 500 to a racer. Preachers want Easter Sunday to be perfect. We want the ushers usherin', the greeters greetin', the choir singin', and the sound man leavin' those little knobs alone. Sometimes it's good for sound men to just go get a cup of coffee.

But things are not always perfect on Easter, however hard we may try. One church had a children's sermon every Sunday, even on Easter. One Easter Sunday the little kids all came and sat at the preacher's feet while he sat on the top steps of the platform. He asked a four-year-old boy what happened on Easter.

The little boy answered, "That's when Jesus came out of the

tomb, saw his shadow, and went back in until winter was over."

That preacher might just as well have ended his service then and there. But I had an Easter experience that makes his look minor.

After a few years in the ministry, you learn to have a sense of humor. I remember when I left First Baptist Church of Rogers to go to First Baptist Church of Saginaw, Texas. What a great ministry I had there. Those fine folks were just seven miles north of Billy Bob's in Fort Worth, the nation's biggest country-western club. They were in Cowtown USA—if you know what I mean.

On Easter Sunday, First Baptist Church of Saginaw was packed. You know how everybody comes to church on Easter. I mean, it was *packed*. Man, I was ready to go. Our girls' high-school basketball coach was there to give his testimony. I was thinking, *Go, baby, go*. People were wall to wall in the sanctuary. I was ready.

Then I noticed water dripping from the ceiling. The condensation pans in the air-conditioning units were overflowing, and water was falling through the ceiling onto the choir loft. Women in the choir were trying to scoot over inconspicuously, but soon everybody felt the thunder. Finally some of the women looked pointedly at their husbands as if to say, *Do somethin' about it*.

Two men got up and went out the side door. I knew they were heading up to the attic to repair the air-conditioning units. They should probably have just turned the broken units off, but they decided to go up there and fix them instead.

They're gonna be heroes, I thought.

We heard them walking above us. Then it happened. Terry's legs came right through the ceiling by the baptistery. His legs waved frantically, trying to step on something, anything. There was nothing for him to step on, so he held on to two-by-sixes for his life.

A gasp rose from the audience, "Oooh, oooooh!"

It just about scared everybody to death. Terry's mama was sitting over in what we call the "afghan division." We always had about three rows full of afghans that some of our women had crocheted. Those who were cold-natured "afghaned up" every service to keep warm. That's where Terry's mom was.

She wailed, "Terrrrrrrry!"

She recognized his flailing, chubby legs. His pants were torn, and he was bleeding. The coach saw him up there, then he turned to look at me.

Only preachers can pray this fast. In that split second, I prayed, "Lord, don't let Coach say something he'd say on the basketball court." Not that he *would,* but he *could.*

All of a sudden Coach said, "Brother Dennis, are we having a healing service? Someone's coming in through the roof."

Everybody just howled with laughter. People love it when something goes wrong in church. Some were even saying, "Man, we ought to come here every Sunday."

It got worse. While Terry was hanging from the ceiling, Ernie, the other guy up there, started talking to him as if we couldn't hear him. He asked Terry, "Can you see anybody?"

Terry looked down and said, "Well, uh, I can see the choir."

Somehow someone pulled him back up into the ceiling. It looked like the bodily Assumption taking place before our Easter eyes. But instead of going up into the clouds, Terry went up into the Sheetrock. A big piece of Sheetrock continued to swing from the ceiling, so when I got up to preach my Easter masterpiece, I looked out at five thousand sets of eyes, all looking up. Did you ever try to preach while everyone's waiting for an usher to fall through the roof again? Well, I gave it my best effort.

I noticed a rancher sitting in the back the whole service. He had a big chew of tobacco, but thankfully he did not spit. I did appreciate that. He was the first one out of the sanctuary, and he came right up to me said, "Brother Dennis, I told my wife there was no need for me to come to church today. I told her if I did, the roof would cave in, and sure enough it did!" Now that's the truth.

FOOD FOR THOUGHT

He is not here; for He is risen, as He said.
—Matthew 28:6

That Easter surprise was nothing compared to the surprise on the first Easter morning. You see, no one expected Jesus Christ to rise from the dead. Not one person among the Jews, Romans, Greeks, or even Jesus' own followers expected him to leave the tomb where his body had been sealed. The Romans had posted a group of seasoned army veterans to guard Jesus' grave. Those four men would pay with their lives if the grave was disturbed. Further, the seal of Rome had been placed on the massive stone that shut Jesus' body inside the tomb. No one messed with the seal of Rome. Yet in spite of all that, the women who visited Jesus' tomb on the first day of the week found that tomb open and empty (see Matthew 28:1–8).

Doubting cynics have always tried to say that someone stole Jesus' body. But if the Romans or the Jews stole it, all they had to do was produce the body when, a few weeks later, they wanted to stop Christianity in its tracks. Did the believers take the body? During the Watergate conspiracy, it took only a few days for John Dean to turn state's evidence and tell his whole story. If the early Christians did take Jesus' body, at least fifteen people had to enter into a lifelong conspiracy to fool the entire human race. Most of them paid for that so-called conspiracy with their lives.

Frank Morrison set out to write a book that would prove for all time that Jesus Christ did not rise from the dead. He intended to present the evidence in such a compelling way that no one would believe in the Resurrection. Instead, as he researched the facts, he was forced to confess the Resurrection in *Who Moved the Stone?*

The biggest surprise of all is the resurrection of Jesus Christ. He went into the raw, red throat of death and emerged as Victor. He broke the chains of death against the stone walls of that sepulcher and triumphed over the last enemy.

Chapter Thirteen

The famous Methodist preacher W. E. Sangster spent his last Easter in silence because his body was ravaged by muscular dystrophy.

His daughter said, "What a terrible thing to know the Easter message and have no voice to tell it."

He summoned her closer so he could whisper, "No. What a terrible thing to know it and not want to tell it."

The Resurrection is the biggest news in history. CNN ought to put it on Headline News every thirty minutes. It should scream from every headline: *Jesus is alive!*

Children were giggling, old ladies were snickering, and the ushers in the back were laughing without reservation.

A CHARMIN' SUNDAY

Every calling has to start somewhere. Some poor old boy was a now-famous surgeon's first patient. Some poor old defendant is sitting in jail somewhere because he was a young lawyer's first case. Some brother has awfully short sideburns because he was a new barber's first customer. And, of course, somebody has to be on board the first time a new pilot lands a jet.

But there is a special group of saints walking the Earth—the folks who help their young pastor with his first pastorate. In a real way they pastor him more than he pastors them. They let him practice preachin', buryin', marryin', baptizin', and holdin' business meetings. I was very blessed by the dear folks in the first church I pastored.

91

🫑 *Chapter Fourteen* 🫑

Serving the Lord in Rogers, Texas, was a marvelous experience. This central Texas town had a population of one thousand and was ideally suited for my sanguine personality. I am an old country boy with an appreciation for down-home folks. The fellowship in Bell County was more than wonderful; it was the foundation for my future as a pastor, Christian humorist, and encourager in the kingdom enterprise of joy. God repeatedly allowed the medicine of laughter to be administered to me during my pastorate in Rogers. One particular incident was truly a "charmin'" experience.

Sunday mornings in Rogers had a routine of their own. For me, it was up and at 'em around 6:00 A.M. I would rise and shine and give God the glory as I brewed some Community Blend, dark roasted, Louisiana coffee. (If you mean business in the ministry, always drink dark roast. It will set you free!) Each Sunday, I pressed onward, upward, and outward as I bolted out of the parsonage, into the car, and on to the church with my Bible in my hand and a message burning in my heart.

As pastor of a small church, I was also supervisor of maintenance and engineering. That meant I made sure all the doors were unlocked and the heating or cooling system was on. I put the bulletins in their places by each entrance. And I checked to make sure all the bathrooms were working. (That was one "overflow" you did not pray for on a Sunday.) I finally took refuge in my office to gather my thoughts. I prayed as I played some soothing, inspiring music on the record player and began to imagine the blessings that were about to be reaped.

I am a person with a positive disposition, and as I envisioned First Baptist Church of Rogers during that 11:00 hour as a high hour of heaven, I could see it—I could feel it. I knew that this particular day was going to be special. There was something wonderful about this particular Sunday, and charmin' would be an understatement.

Soon I saw a white truck pull into the parking lot—it was longtime church member and a pastor's best friend, Doyle Ray. In season and out of season, Doyle was there with a smile and an encouraging word for this green, "wet behind the ears" preacher.

As the Sunday-school superintendent, Doyle would see to it that everything was in order for Sunday classes. He was a pro! He was also a successful paint contractor and could legitimately be labeled a bivocational minister. He and his wife, Aubrey, had been faithful to their church for more than thirty years. Together we made sure all the coffeepots were full and hot. (Baptists must have their daily dose of caffeine in order to hear the Word and act on it. How shall they hear without a cup of dark roast in their Styrofoam cups?)

The congregation slowly began entering the hallowed, cedar halls. Sunday school was scheduled to start at 9:30, but the first fifteen minutes always served as a Baptist "happy hour" for fellowship and catching up on local news. Finally, around 9:45, God began to move his people to the spiritual things of Sunday. Like the great exodus of the Old Testament, people crossed over into the classrooms, took their seats, and listened to announcements.

Soon the people were into the Word. As I walked down the halls, I could hear Bible teaching in every classroom. Discussions were in line with the day's lesson. Proudly, I went back to my office to go over my three main points and a poem. I was pumped! Attendance was better than usual (one of our ushers had completed the car/truck count, and it was above average). It was a Baptist banner day, and I was excited about the offering. Because it was the first Sunday of the month, I knew it could be a good "nickel and noses" day. (That's preacher terminology for big offering and big attendance.)

I looked at my watch—10:45. *Start your engines, Swan. It's time.* Pacing my office as usual, I began to pray again for the Lord's mercy and grace. I prayed for patience, power, and perseverance as I preached. I prayed for souls. I prayed for heaven to come down and touch all these charmin' people.

I could hear beautiful organ music, and by the sounds I knew it was our own beloved Faith Keith tiptoeing through each tune. I could also hear Beverly Ralston "tickling the ivories" at the piano. These two were a dynamite duo on Sunday mornings. Buoyed by their music, I stepped into the choir room to encourage the choir, who was robing up. I had followed this routine every Sunday, but on this day I had to cut my visit to the choir room short because of the "call of nature." I went quickly into the rest room, hurrying so I could walk into the church behind the choir.

94

But just a moment later I could hear them leaving me! I couldn't believe it. Every Sunday I waited on the choir because I thought it looked good for us to walk in together. Could they not wait on me? They knew that I was in the rest room—we were family; our walls had no insulation, no soundproof technology—but they took off without me anyway.

I hurried as fast as I could. I opened the bathroom door and hooked 'em to catch up with the choir. I joined up just as the last choir member walked through the door. The choir took its place, and I took mine. Standing on the platform with my Bible in hand, I began to scan the crowd. Everyone was attentive. All eyes were on me. I had them in the palm of my hand. I felt special.

Then I noticed that their attention was more than just a stare. Their countenances were glowing. Children were giggling, old ladies were snickering, and the ushers in the back were laughing without reservation.

I turned to my wife and noticed that she was turning pale. By now, giggling, laughter, and snorting had erupted across the congregation. I knew something was wrong. My mama didn't raise a fool.

From the look on my wife's face, I traced my disgrace to my zipper. *Oh no, not my zipper.* The professors at the seminary had repeatedly instructed us that the last thing you check before going out to the podium is your zipper! *Always* make sure it is up and in the locked position.

I turned to my left and looked into the face of our music minister, Coleman Young. Coleman was a spry seventy-year-old who had survived World War II and endured the Texas heat, but he had only a pathetic look for me. The helpless expression on his face said, *Swan, you're on your own. I can't help you. There's not enough music in all of central Texas to overshadow this exposé.*

I looked to my right and saw our college minister, Scott Bryant. He was spellbound one minute and laughing uproariously the next. Everyone seemed to be amused, except me.

I boldly decided to take my medicine. I slowly, methodically, and ashamedly looked down at my zipper. It was up and in the locked position. But then I looked down at my shoe and saw a six-foot piece of Charmin toilet tissue! What do you do in that situation? I just whipped it around my leg and stayed behind the pulpit for the rest of the service.

It was a "charmin'" Sunday I will never forget.

FOOD FOR THOUGHT

He had to be made like His brethren, that He might be a merciful and faithful High Priest.

—Hebrews 2:17

A preacher always needs to let his people know that he is with them, for them, and one of them. We preachers need to embrace our humanity. When God wanted to redeem the world, he sent his Son in the form of a human, not an angel. More than ever people need to know that preachers are one of them.

Several years ago a woman from Washington state visited

Washington, D.C. She was so moved by the plight of the street people that she decided to do something about it. She went back home with her husband and children but later returned to Washington, D.C., dressed as a bag lady. She lived among the street people and found out what it was like to have no food, no home, and no money. She wrote a vivid account of her experience that helped change the circumstances of such people. That is an incarnation of love.

Preachers, like all Christians, are best when they incarnate the love of God among their people. Sometimes that means leaving a paper trail—literally. That makes people love them all the more because it shows they are just like everyone else, imperfect humans saved by grace.

I was young in the ministry. I wondered, How am I going to do this? Do I grab her by the hair and just yank her down?

Chapter 15

BAPTISMAL
DRAIN

Some churches sprinkle, but we Baptists dunk our converts. And we don't just dunk children; we submerge three-hundred-pound truck drivers in front of hundreds of people. And we have to do it with dignity.

One of my favorite professors at Baylor University was Dr. Richard Cutter. He tried to teach us preacher boys a little Greek. (Most of us thought a little Greek ran the restaurant across from Brooks Hall. But we tried.) Dr. Cutter informed us that the Greek verb *baptizo* meant to put something under water. When Herodotus, the father of history, wrote about a boat that sank under the ocean waters, he used the word *baptizo*. That sucker went all the way under, and so should we, said Dr. Cutter. Armed with such esoteric knowledge and great learning, we boys fanned out across Texas to *baptizo* as many folks as we could. We figured they needed to be dunked, and besides, that's how Baptists keep score.

We had some memorable baptismal services at the mighty First Baptist Church of Rogers, Texas. I can remember them vividly. Our beautiful baptismal pool featured a mural that one of our ladies painted on the back wall of the baptistery. It was a lovely picture of Jesus and John the Baptist, with a twist—they have blond hair, blue eyes, and are standing in the Brazos River in central Texas. What always got me tickled were the sheep and armadillos painted in the backdrop.

One little lady said, "I think the mural adds so much to the service."

I responded truthfully, "It does add somethin', I'll admit."

At one baptismal service, the baptistery was too full of water. I think this happens at least once to just about every Baptist preacher. When I submerged the baptismal candidate, the water went up and went over the glass partition and splashed the choir.

You know how choir people are: "I've got water all over my robe. My robe is ruined! It's ruined! It's robe number forty-three. Look at robe number forty-three after the service. It's absolutely ruined."

Later the deacons got together and said, "Brother Dennis, let us handle this for you. Let us be a buffer for you. It's a sensitive issue."

I said, "It is? Just a little water?"

They nodded solemnly. "Trust us. It's a *sssensitive* issue."

To fix the baptistery, they put a drainage pipe three inches below the top of the glass in the back left corner of the baptismal pool. If the water ever got too high again, instead of going over the glass, it would go down the rear drainage pipe.

The next person I baptized was a "mature" woman— "mature" in every area of life. She got on into the baptistery with me. Now, I'm a good-sized fellow myself, and with the two of us in there, the water level started going up. I saw people making faces on the other side of the glass.

The ushers in the back started waving their arms and warning, "It's goin' over. It's goin' over."

But water didn't go over the glass. The water level went up, but the water started spilling down that drainage pipe just like they'd planned. But have you ever heard water being sucked down a drainage pipe? It is the worst slurping sound you have ever heard in your life. I quickly took my left hand and tried to squelch it as best I could. But that only left me with one arm to baptize this mature woman.

I was young in the ministry. I wondered, *How am I going to do this? Do I grab her by the hair and just yank her down?*

I knew she would eventually come up. People are buoyant. They'll always bob right on up. It's getting them under the water that's hard.

Usually I have people cross their arms. Then I put my hand behind their head and do a chiropractic *whomp* move on them to get them all the way under. I hate to baptize people, bring them up, and discover a dry patch on their foreheads. That's what makes men go bald.

So there I was with my left hand over the drain pipe. I started to get worried. *How am I going to baptize this woman?*

Finally, I got an idea, and I whispered, "Could you squat down?"

She apparently didn't know that women are supposed to be quiet in the church. She repeated loudly, *"Squat?"*

I said, "Could you squat on down just a little? If you love Jesus, if you love your mama, please squat on down!"

So she squatted down as far as she could squat. Water came to about her lip.

"Could you squat down just a little farther?"

"Squat? I am squattin'! I have squatted as far as I can squat!"

I didn't know what to do. So I just reverted to my Methodist roots and splashed water on the rest of her.

FOOD FOR THOUGHT

If anyone is in Christ, he is a new creation.
—2 Corinthians 5:17

A lot of funny stories gather around the baptismal pool. If we're not careful, we can forget how significant baptism really is.

Years ago, the famous preacher Robert G. Lee traveled to the Holy Land and asked a little Arab boy to take him to the top of Calvary. The little boy took the famous old preacher to the top of the hill. Dr. Lee just stood there for a long time.

The little boy finally asked, "Mister, have you been here before?"

You can imagine how surprised that little boy was when Dr. Lee said, "Yes, lad, I was here two thousand years ago." The boy must have thought that Dr. Lee was the oldest man in history.

But when we are baptized, we confess that we were with Christ Jesus in his death, burial, and resurrection. Watchman Nee, in *The Normal Christian Life,* explained this truth simply:

> If I put a letter inside a book, the letter goes where the book goes. If I drop the book, the letter drops. If I mail the book across the world, the letter goes. If I put the book high on a shelf, the letter is high on the shelf. Baptism reminds us of this. We are in Christ. When he died, we died. When he rose, we rose. While he is now in the presence of God, we are in the presence of God. Baptism reminds us that we are in Christ and Christ in us, just like the bird is in the air and air is in the bird, the fish is in water and the water is in the fish.

As a Christian, my most important identity is that I am *in Christ.* Funny things can happen at baptisms, but the greatest fun of all is the joy of being in Christ!

Our deacons felt led to schedule the evening service at 3:00 on Super Bowl Sunday.

Chapter

ROTEL AND RELAXATION

Have you noticed how much we rush around these days? With voice mail, faxes, e-mail, beepers, and cellular phones, no one is ever out of touch. Thanks to FedEx and Airborne Express, you can get anything anywhere in the world overnight. Through the Internet, you can get information on anything from anywhere, immediately—and now they're trying to make the Internet even faster. Everybody wants everything *yesterday*. You can even get shot for driving too slowly on a freeway. And Lord help anybody who dares to go through the "Ten Items, Cash Only" line of the grocery store with eleven items. That could cause a lawsuit from the next guy in line.

Chapter Sixteen

We're all in such a hurry! I once heard about an old man who was so impatient that he had three pet doors cut into his back door.

A friend asked him, "Why do you have three pet doors? Isn't one enough?"

He replied, "I have three cats."

His buddy asked, "Why can't they all use one door?"

"Because when I want them out, I want them out *now.*"

Life moves pretty fast for preachers too. When we aren't preaching, we're in committee meetings. My favorite definition of a committee should be remembered by every preacher: It's a group of people who individually can do nothing but collectively can decide nothing can be done.

Baptist preachers are very busy people. They have to preach a lot: Sunday mornings, Sunday nights, Wednesday nights, weekly Bible studies, funerals, weddings, revivals, and camps. Once I dreamed I was preaching. I woke up and discovered I actually *was* preaching.

I like the story about a man who refused to get up and go to church. His wife tried everything she could to get him out of bed. "Please get up and go to church, honey," she pleaded.

He gave her every excuse under the sun: The people are unfriendly, the services are boring, all they want is money, the church is full of politics, no one at the church liked him anyway, and on and on he went.

"Please get up and go today, honey," she begged one more time when he stopped to take a breath.

"Just give me one good reason why I should get up and go," he retorted.

"Well, honey, for starters, you're the pastor."

You've got to have a sense of humor.

I was pastor of First Baptist Church of West Monroe, Louisiana, for a while. It's a great church, and God did great things there. On Super Bowl Sunday, we scheduled our evening worship service a little earlier so we could all get home in time to watch the game. Our deacons felt led to schedule the evening service at 3:00 on Super Bowl Sunday, and I contend that the Bible says if two are in agreement, so be it. As it was the chairman and the vice-chairman of the deacons who suggested the time change, the motion passed.

And so, on a Sunday night, I got to go home and not work. It was fantastic to be home on Sunday night. To see an entire football game on a Sunday was a dream. We preachers never get to see an entire football game on a Sunday. That's why we love Monday night football. On Sundays we meet to eat, eat to meet, and meet till we're beat all day long.

I went home that Sunday afternoon with a big old grin. I put on my blue jeans and a football jersey that said "The Boys Are Back," then I settled in, turned on the television, and held the remote control. Men love remote controls. They will take it around the block, just checking everything out. When I get old and am put in a rest home, all I'll need is a television and a remote control. Give me a fresh battery every two or three days, and I'll be a happy camper.

Chapter Sixteen

So there I was, sitting in my favorite chair, watching the Super Bowl, and I thought, *Man, this is great.* Every man deserves one special piece of furniture in his home. I've got a blue leather chair with a matching blue ottoman—real leather.

All of a sudden my little sugar babe, Lauree, came into the room and said, "Baby love."

I said, "Honey love, yeah?"

"Would you like some Rotel cheese dip?"

"Baby, you know what I like!"

Lauree makes Rotel cheese dip just right. She doesn't get it out of a jar. She takes the Velveeta block and melts it down in the double boiler. She watches it and stirs it carefully, keeping an eye out for any lumps or burned cheese. Some people try to hide the burned lumps and whip them back in there. Not my woman. Lauree watches it so those burned lumps never get in there. Then she puts in the Rotel and blends it all together.

She brought me a big bowl of Rotel cheese dip and a bag of Doritos chips—the *original* Doritos chips, not that fancy flavored stuff. Then she brought me a plastic cup, double thickness so it doesn't sweat and I can set it wherever I want. She put Diet Coke in my cup because I am concerned about my figure. I took a chip and dragged it through my bowl of cheese dip. I mean, it was the perfect texture. I lifted it up, all wonderful and gooey, and put the whole thing in my mouth. *This is what heaven is like*, I thought.

My wife looked at me and said, "Baby love, you seem so

relaxed. I never see you like this on a Sunday night. You're just so relaxed, so happy, so at peace."

I said, "Baby, do you think this is why they don't come back to church on Sunday night?"

Preach it, Swan, preach it.

FOOD FOR THOUGHT

Come aside by yourselves to a deserted place and rest a while.
—Mark 6:31

Will Rogers used to say, "The government builds the roads in Oklahoma, and the Baptists wear them out going to meetings."

We all need to rest occasionally. One reason so much American Christianity is a mile wide and an inch deep is that Christians are simply tired. Sometimes you need to kick back and rest for Jesus' sake. Some of his most appealing words are found in Matthew 11:28: "Come to Me, all you who labor and are heavy laden, and I will give you rest."

Jesus never said that you had to have a compunction to go to every function until you lose all your unction. When things got busy and stressful, Jesus told his disciples, "Come aside by yourselves to a deserted place and rest a while" (Mark 6:31). Vance Havner used to say, "You will either go apart with him or you will come apart yourself."

Sometimes we just need to be still. Blaise Pascal, the great mathematician and devout Christian, wrote that "half the problems in the world could be solved if men would simply sit quietly in a room, alone for a while."

Isaiah gave one of the grandest promises of all: "Those who wait on the LORD shall renew their strength" (40:31). It's great to be one of Jehovah's waiters—that's what Isaiah literally says. Lots of times we keep going when God says rest. But we can just wait for him to give the word. God will exchange our emptiness for his fullness, our poverty for his resources, and our weakness for his energy.

They were all roaring with laughter. There was nothing I could do but stand up and acknowledge that I had missed the mark.

"YOU'RE ON THE WRONG SIDE!"

During the eighties a phrase became popular in busy, harassed families. Parents began to speak of "quality time." The scam went something like this: Just as long as you spend a few *quality* minutes with your kids—totally focused on them, giving them your full attention—it really doesn't matter whether you spend any *quantity* of time with them. The problem is, that just doesn't wash. If you don't believe me, take a look at nature.

Try telling a giant sequoia redwood tree, "It really doesn't take any quantity of time to be a redwood. It just takes a little quality time." Of course, that's not true. The oldest, tallest, and most durable trees take *time* to grow and develop. That is why people visit the giant redwoods; they can see the difference time makes.

Ask an oyster if it can make a pearl with *quality* time. The oyster will assure you that it takes a long time to make a pearl.

The fact is, the things we really value take time. No one can become a concert pianist, a professional golfer, or a brain surgeon without time to learn and practice. No one can build a baseball-card collection or a career overnight. The most valued of all gemstones starts as carbon. After being subjected to pressure thousands of feet beneath the earth for thousands of years, it becomes a beautiful diamond.

Why in the world would we imagine that our kids do not need our time? Kids are observant. They know whether you are there for them. I have living proof of that.

I love my boys, and I love to see them play Dixie youth baseball. In West Monroe, Louisiana, we had the best program, in my opinion, in the whole country. My boys loved baseball. Little Dusty enjoyed it, too, even though it was sort of hard for him to focus at times because he has attention deficit disorder (ADD).

When coaches have a player with ADD on the team, they don't put that kid in the infield because kids with ADD don't pay attention in practice. So coaches tend to put the kid in the outfield. The problem is, when a kid like that gets in the outfield and it's hard for him to focus on the game, the next thing you know he's out there in left field doing the Ninja Turtle or Karate Kid or digging a hole in the ground to make a fort, like he's going to have his own little war out there. That's where my Dusty was, because he's just like his daddy. He's got ADD; therefore, he's out there in left field.

I got to the ball game just as it was about to start. I was going to have to leave after the first inning because I had a speaking engagement. We preachers have a hard time saying no to other churches, so we tend to overextend ourselves, sometimes even to the neglect of our own families. I admit it. I am a sinner, and I've missed the mark many times. In spite of that, I was at Dusty's game, and I wanted to see as much as I could.

I got out of my car, took off my coat, and loosened my tie. I wanted to look like a regular dad, not a pastor. I made my way to the ballpark and greeted some of the folks. I found my way over to the third base side and climbed up into the bleachers. As I climbed, I shook a lot of folks' hands and introduced myself. These days not that many moms and dads attend the games regularly, so I didn't know most of the folks. I wished the game would get started, but the coaches were going over the rules with the umpires.

Meanwhile, I was thinking, *Let's get this thing going. Come on now. Let's get three up, three down and go in and bat a little bit. If I can see Dusty bat, then I can sneak out.*

As I was sitting up there in the bleachers waiting for the game to get under way, there was a lull. Everyone was waiting for the umpire to say, "Play ball."

All of a sudden from the left field my little Dusty screamed at the top of his lungs, "Daddy, you're sitting on the wrong side!"

Everybody laughed.

I looked around and thought, *What's the matter with that boy? What does he mean I'm on the wrong side?*

I looked over to the bleachers on the first base side and, sure enough, there were all the moms and dads I knew. There were the players I knew. And they were all roaring with laughter. There was nothing I could do but stand up and acknowledge that I had missed the mark. I said good-bye to the folks in the third base bleachers and walked down the steps as if I were rededicating my life at a Billy Graham crusade. I was humbled going down those bleachers, walking behind the backstop, and making my way over to the first-base side. I made my way up into the bleachers—and received a standing ovation. I sat down, embarrassed.

I looked out at Dusty, and he gave me a "thumbs-up" from left field. Dusty had nailed his daddy. I really couldn't blame him—I *was* on the wrong side. But he was happy again now that I had found my designated position.

We were three up and three down. As Dusty made his way to the dugout, he ran across the field just beaming, looking up at his daddy with his eyes all aglow. He obviously loved that his daddy was there. I realized then that kids look up to us more than we think they do. They want us to always be there for them. Dusty was about the fifth batter. He was kicking at the bat with his feet just like he was a professional baseball player, and he was spitting everywhere. When it was time for him to get up to the batter's box, he walked up there like Ol'

Casey at the plate. He stood in the batter's box and looked over to see if I was watching. He gave me a big grin, loving the attention.

Dusty ripped one out to center field. He ran down the first base line while looking up into the bleachers proudly, took the turn at first base, and then got back on the base. He just kept beaming.

I was fired up and yelled, "Way to go, Dusty! Rip it! Way to run, son!"

I was proud of my son. Then he stole second base. The batter got a hit, and Dusty ran to third base and on to home plate. He didn't need to slide, but he slid anyway. He got dirt all over his uniform—I knew that would make his mama happy. As he ran back to the dugout, he held his helmet in his hand and looked at me, just glowing and smiling.

I was so glad I got to see that, but I knew I had to leave. I sneaked down the steps as though I were going to get some popcorn, mingled a little, and then tried to slip out inconspicuously to the parking lot. I got in my car and had to hook 'em to make it to the banquet on time.

The whole way to the banquet, I could hear Dusty's voice like an echo in my heart and soul, "Daddy, you're sitting on the wrong side!" I heard it over and over again in my mind. Even as I write this story, I can still hear him.

But then I remembered how he gave me a "thumbs-up" when I saw the error of my ways and moved. Kids are so forgiving. No wonder God wants us to be as children. Our little ones who love us so much always want to see us on the right side: They want us to be on the right side with God; they want us to be on the right side with our spouse; they want to see us on the right side with our children, family, and friends; they even want to see us on the right side of the baseball field, with their team, the natural place for them to look for us.

Since that game, I have tried to reevaluate where I am in the lives of my boys. Sometimes I hear the echo, "Daddy, you're sitting on the wrong side." Sometimes I get a "thumbs-up." I hope we will always be on the right side with our heavenly Father and with our families and families of faith.

FOOD FOR THOUGHT

Because you are sons, God has sent forth the Spirit of His Son into your hearts, crying out, "Abba, Father!"
—Galatians 4:6

Every boy needs a dad. Jesus chose the word *Abba*, the Aramaic word for "Daddy," to describe God. No one before Jesus had ever used that word when speaking of God. Jesus meant that God is more like a father than anything else we can imagine him to be. God is not like a dictator, a king, or a president; he is like a father.

Best-selling author Thomas Moore in his *Care of the Soul* emphasizes how much each of us needs a father in the earthly sense. Unfortunately, life does not give everyone a good father. In such cases, Moore emphasizes that we must seek father figures, paternalistic friends who are father substitutes. So great is our need for a father that we literally cannot survive without one.

It is little wonder that the greatest prayer ever prayed begins with the words, "Our Father…" (Matthew 6:9). Jesus' dying words were, "Father, into Your hands I commend My spirit" (Luke 23:46). We all need a Father, and we need to be good fathers who get a "thumbs-up" from our loved ones as well as from the perfect Father. I hope we're all sitting on the right side.

It doesn't matter how you
say "I love you" as long
as you say it.

Chapter 18

"HOW ABOUT THOSE COWBOYS?"

A lot of people have asked the question: "How do I say 'I love you'?" Florists want you to say it with flowers. Jewelers want you to say it with diamonds.

Elizabeth Barrett Browning asked, "How do I love thee? Let me count the ways." For years, Elizabeth Barrett had been an invalid, bedfast in her room. The first time Robert Browning came to visit her, she sat up. The second time he visited, she walked around the room. The third time, they eloped. How's that for the power of love?

My oldest son, Chad, took adolescence by storm! By the time we moved from the pastorate at First Baptist Church of West Monroe, Louisiana, to Southwestern Baptist Theological Seminary where I became the special assistant to the president

121

in seminary relations, Chad was full-bloom into puberty. (No, that's not a style of music—although Chad was just hitting the "B-natural" chord. The vibrations were taking years off my life.) Nevertheless, Chad and I continued to bond as father and son as we shared our points of view with each other.

I remember when Chad decided I was using the phrase "I love you" too often in public. It especially bothered him when I said it around his buddies, creatures of his same kind. It seemed as though mutation was manifesting itself before my very eyes.

Sadly enough, one night Chad said, "Dad, we need to find a code phrase to say 'I love you' instead of actually saying it." I listened quietly as he explained that we could have a phrase like the father and son on the television sitcom *Home Improvement*. He told me the dad would say, "How about those [Detroit] Tigers?" as an incognito way of saying "I love you."

I couldn't believe this was happening to the Swan. I have always verbalized my love to my boys. Many men have trouble saying "I love you," and I really believe our children need to hear these words often. But Chad had heard them often enough. He wanted me to be more like other dads.

So "preacher" dad backed off and said, "Okay, what should our code be?"

Chad suggested, "How about those Cowboys?"

I conceded. That night as I tucked him in—excuse me—said good night to him, I simply said, "Sleep well, son, and uh, 'How about those Cowboys?'"

Chad gave me a high-five, and that was that.

I walked down the hall, fell into my big blue chair, and muttered, "How about those Cowboys?" I didn't feel like I had made a first down. Instead, I felt like I had gotten a fifteen-yard penalty for being a dad on the cutting edge. My offensive strategy was out of sync, and the game plan was going to a preventive defense rather than an aggressive attack on the gridiron of fatherhood. I would have to wait for that hug and "I love you." I was a bit jealous of Lauree. She still had a full-fledged and dominating offense. She still received the hugs and "I love you's" of her older teenaged son.

I longed for expressions of love with my boys. I knew, however, that I needed to understand Chad's language of love. I had to learn to be bilingual with a son going through the change of adolescence.

Then George Strait came to Shreveport, Louisiana, to give a concert; I'll never be the same. He may not know it, but I believe God brought him to our state.

When Lauree found out about the concert in Shreveport, she immediately bought tickets for our entire family. Lauree loves George Strait. So do Chad and Dusty. And I must confess, I like him too. We are a country-western music family. But the concert was an hour-and-a-half drive from West Monroe, and it was on a Saturday evening. I usually try to rest and polish my sermon on the night before the Lord's day, but that Saturday night, we dressed in western apparel and prepared to go to the concert.

Lauree pulled out all the stops with her outfit. I never knew a preacher's wife could be so good looking! Lauree was the Barbara Mandrell of ministers' wives. The Swan was decked out too. I was the Garth Brooks of Baptists. I had on my ostrich boots, and my belt had a shiny new buckle with a huge *S* on it.

I wanted to leave early enough to get some seafood in Shreveport and still have time to choose a good seat for the concert. I said, "Let's get going. Let's crank it on out. Come on, Mama, you can redo your lipstick in the car."

We finally pulled into the parking lot and still had a half-mile walk to the coliseum. I took off, leading the pack, walking several steps ahead of the family. Lauree called to me, and I looked back but didn't see Chad. He was behind a Suburban. He had just lost his deluxe shrimp dinner. Evidently the excitement was too much for him. Lauree mouthed to me not to say a word.

Oh, he'll be all right, I thought. *I'll get him some popcorn, a hot dog, and nachos. He'll be as good as new.*

When we entered the coliseum, it was packed with every country-western music lover from the regions of Texas, Arkansas, and North Louisiana. Looking at how everyone was dressed, one would have thought that the best-dressed cowboy and cowgirl would win a backstage pass to hang out with George.

Down the hallway was a cardboard cutout of George Strait. We took our camera out of its holster and persuaded a Dolly Parton look-alike to take our picture with George. I love that picture. We were having fun. It was the first time that our entire family looked like we were not in the ministry. I felt like a tenured usher on a mission to stardom in country music.

Lauree was singing along to "Amarillo by Morning," and I found myself thinking, *Will they call it preaching when I deliver the sermon tomorrow morning?*

While Chad and Dusty began harmonizing to "All My Exes Live in Texas," I started looking for the nearest exit. I was thinking about how to get out of there quick enough to beat the traffic for the long drive home. I finally got into the concert when George started singing about the Heartland. I stopped worrying and started laughing, singing, and having a good time.

Just then Chad leaned over, put his arm around me, and said, "Dad, how about those Cowboys?"

Touchdown! We embraced and turned our attention back to George.

Then it hit me. It doesn't matter how you say "I love you" as long as you say it. Chad's language of love suddenly became my own. We had the joy of communicating that special love.

I stood tall that night. I sang, laughed, and almost cried. In that moment, the Lord spoke to my heart, *How about that, cowboy?*

FOOD FOR THOUGHT

This is My commandment, that you love one another as I have loved you.
—John 15:12

There are many ways to say "I love you." The Greeks had several words for love. The word *storge* was the kind of love

125

you feel for the old pair of house shoes that your wife wants to throw away but you want to keep. It's what you mean when you say, "I love Blue Bell Ice Cream."

The Greeks also used the word *eros*. That, loosely translated, means "Hubba, hubba, come to me, baby."

Then there was *philos*, the love of friendship. That's the love two good buddies who share a deer lease for years or like to fish together every Saturday feel for each other. It's the bond of having something in common.

Highest of all is *agape*, the love of God. This love creates value in the object of the love. It is the love of Calvary. The great old Lutheran scholar R. C. H. Linski said that *agape* always seeks the highest good of the loved one. That is God's kind of love. Share it often.

Part Three

LAU
GH
ING
WITH OUR
FRIENDS

"Help! I've been shot, and my brains are coming out of my head!"

Chapter 19

BISCUIT DOUGH

After speaking in Columbia, South Carolina, I had a sweet lady come up to me with a great story about her daughter's best friend. This unbelievable story eventually made the local evening news. I have changed the names and "Swanized" it for your enjoyment.

One hot, summer day, Debbie decided to stop by the grocery store to pick up a handful of things. After checking out at the register, she headed out to the parking lot.

She walked in a determined manner toward her car, glancing from side to side occasionally, watching for suspicious cars and people. As she reached her car, she noticed an elderly woman slumped over the steering wheel in the car next to hers! Startled, she approached the other car.

Peering into the window, Debbie knocked on the glass and asked, "Lady, are you okay?"

The woman, still slumped over the wheel, said, "Help me! I've been shot in the back of my head!"

Debbie couldn't believe it. She tried not to panic. In one swift motion, she set down her groceries, pulled out her portable phone, and dialed 9-1-1. She told the operator about the crisis and gave their location.

The operator professionally responded, "Stay with her. Help is on the way!"

Debbie tried to peer through the car window, but the afternoon sun reflecting off the glass caused quite a glare. She thought, *If I could just unlock her doors, I could do more for her. Oh, help me, Jesus!*

Again, she knocked on the glass and said, "Ma'am, move your left hand and release the lock so I can help you."

The frozen little lady, still staring blindly, wailed, "I've been shot in the back of the head! My brains are coming out behind my ear!"

Debbie tried all the doors with no luck—they were all locked. She was frantic. She cupped her hands around her face to reduce the sun's glare and peered into the driver's window. She looked behind the lady's ear to deduce the severity of her gunshot wound. Suddenly, Debbie's countenance changed completely.

The little lady again moaned, "Help! I've been shot, and my brains are coming out of my head!"

A very perturbed Debbie responded, "Lady, you have not been shot. The heat caused a can of biscuit dough in your sack to explode and hit your head. That is *biscuit dough* behind your ear, not brains! You haven't been shot at all!"

A can of biscuit dough. From this day forward, when I open up one of those cans I'm going to think, *Perspective. Balance. All in Jesus.*

FOOD FOR THOUGHT

Be still, and know that I am God.
—Psalm 46:10

There are times when more than anything else we need the calm that only God can bring. In the forty-sixth psalm we read the awesome command: "Be still, and know that I am God" (v. 10). Psalm 46 presents a calamity not unlike the biscuit-dough scene but with more serious overtones. The psalmist's entire world seemed to turn upside down in a moment. He described his turmoil in poetic terminology: The earth quaked beneath his feet. The mountains toppled over into the sea. The sea itself seemed as if it would overtake the dry land. What in the world would the psalmist do?

God remains silent until the tenth verse of the psalm. Then God says, "Be still." The original Hebrew literally means, "Let your hands hang down." We are always throwing our hands up in frustration, confusion, or hurry. But God says, "Let your hands hang down." In other words, be calm and submissive to God. Be silent. Be still.

This is the same thing Paul referred to in the famous promise of Philippians 4:7: "The peace of God, which surpasses all understanding, will guard your hearts and minds through Christ Jesus."

When we submit difficult and alarming situations to God, he promises that his peace will be like a military garrison to guard our hearts from fear. The very heavenly hosts of God will guard the hearts of his people when they submit their frightening situations to him.

The next time you encounter a "can of biscuit dough" that could lead to a panic attack, stand back and submit that situation in all of its fearful parts to God. He will make good on his promise.

She remembered what
he'd done the night before
and just couldn't resist
the urge.

ZIPPER REVENGE

Things are not always what they seem. Some friends of mine discovered this in a dramatic way they'll never forget.

My dear friends Benji and Connie are also in the ministry. They're of my own kind. Remember, we in the ministry are just normal, regular people. We're God-called, but we're regular. We're sinners just like everybody else, and we sometimes have little tiffs and tough times in our marriages. I know my sugar babe and I do. I don't like to call them arguments, just "discussions."

Ol' Benji and Connie had a little "discussion" one day. She just didn't think he helped out enough. They had a formal banquet that night at church, and neither Benji nor Connie felt like going to the banquet in the middle of a tiff, but they had no choice. He was on staff and had to be there. They were just going to have to fake it the whole night and pretend that everything was fine.

Connie put on her formal dress. It had a long zipper that extended from the waist all the way to the neck. She couldn't get it all the way up, so she asked Benji with a ticked-off tone of voice, "Do you think you could manage to help me with the zipper? Can you at least do that much?"

Old Benji muttered, "Yeah, I can do it."

He grabbed that zipper and thought, *While I'm at it, I'll have a little fun.* He went zzzzz zzzzzz zzzzzz, zipping up and down, up and down. All of a sudden, the pull tab of the zipper broke off.

Connie was hot. "You did *not* just break my zipper!"

They had to be at the dinner in less than fifteen minutes.

Benji said, "I can fix it."

So he got some pliers and pushed and pried, but he couldn't fix it. She had to pin the dress closed and put on a shawl to cover the pins—in the middle of June.

She wailed, "I'm so embarrassed. It's summer, and I have to wear the shawl my grandmother made."

Benji tried to comfort her. "Well, you look good, baby."

They got in the car and drove to the church in absolute silence. But as soon as they got there, they put on their social smiles and started greeting people.

Benji kept saying, "Doesn't Connie look great?"

All the ladies said, "Oh, Connie, your shawl looks really nice."

She said, "Well my grandmother made it, and I knew it would be cold in here tonight. It's always so cold in the church. I thought I'd wear it just to keep warm."

"Good idea, Connie. Wish I had one."

So they made it through the whole evening. But when they got in the car to go home, Connie wailed, "I have never been so humiliated in my whole life!"

"Honey, everybody was saying how great you look."

"They were lying. They were just being Christian."

When they got home, Benji and Connie went straight to bed. She slept on her side, and he slept on his. They did not pass go; they did not collect two hundred dollars—you understand what I'm saying. The next morning, Connie woke up first and got dressed. Then she woke Benji.

He mumbled sleepily, "Where you going, Connie?"

"Benji, I'm going shopping. I'm gonna buy me two formals and charge them on the credit card. I don't care what Larry Burkett and Ron Blue say."

"Go ahead, be a bad steward if you want to."

She marched out of the house, bought herself two dresses, and came back later that afternoon. When she pulled up, she saw old Benji underneath his car just working his heart out. He appeared to be changing the oil.

She got out with her bags and looked at him indignantly. She could just see the lower half of his body; the rest of him was underneath the car. As she looked down and saw Benji's zipper, she remembered what he'd done the night before and just couldn't resist the urge. So she put her bags down, grabbed the zipper tab on his pants, and went zzzzzz zzzzzz zzzzz up and down, up and down, up and down. Satisfied with her revenge, she picked up her bags, walked inside, and put her bags on the kitchen table. As she walked back into the den, she saw Benji watching television.

She gasped, and the color drained from her face.

Benji said, "Connie, baby. Look, I'm sorry about the dress. I'm *really* sorry."

"I don't care about the dress, Benji! *Who is underneath our car?*"

"Old Bubba from next door. He changed the oil in his car and said, while he was at it, he would change the oil in ours too."

Connie started to sob uncontrollably, horrified.

"What's the matter, baby?"

She confessed what she had done.

"You did not! *You did not!*"

"I thought it was you," she wept.

Then Connie looked at her husband and demanded, "You go out there and do something to fix this. And you'd better not let him know it was me!"

So Benji went outside. Bubba was still underneath the car.

Benji said, "Hey, Bubba, come on out. I need to talk to you."

Bubba didn't move.

Benji squatted down and looked underneath the car. Bubba was out cold.

He pulled Bubba out, slapped him on the cheek, and said, "Bubba! Hey, Bubba! Wake up!"

Bubba rubbed his forehead and stammered, "Benji, you're not going to believe this! I was putting the last twist on your oil filter and a woman came right up to me, grabbed my pants zipper, and started zipping it up and down. Scared me half to death. I jumped up to see who it was, and I must have hit my head on the oil pan and knocked myself out."

Benji said, "Oh, I've heard about that crazy woman—she lives way down the street! Way down the street!"

FOOD FOR THOUGHT

Let every man be swift to hear, slow to speak, slow to wrath.
—James 1:19

What a story of mistaken identity! Shakespeare would have a hard time matching that in any of his comedies. Yet things that are funny often hide a deeper truth. Humor has a way of getting us close to reality. God told the prophet Samuel, "The LORD does not see as man sees; for man looks at the outward appearance, but the LORD looks at the heart" (1 Samuel 16:7).

We live in an age when almost every judgment we make is quick and superficial. We measure our worth by the latest looks, the most recent buzzwords, the coolest songs, and the wildest stars. But God is not impressed with any of those things. A national magazine recently devoted a cover story to what makes people beautiful. It concluded that beautiful people have symmetrical faces; in other words, both sides match exactly. It showed a picture of poor old Lyle Lovett with his face reimaged symmetrically by a computer, and he looked like a different man. But, are asymmetrical faces really our main problem?

Not at all. Our main problem isn't external; it's internal. We need to learn how to look past a person's face and into a person's heart. Benji and Connie got over their little squabble because they could look into each other's hearts. James, the half-brother of Jesus, wrote some good advice about jumping to conclusions: "Let every man be swift to hear, slow to speak, slow to wrath" (1:19).

Jumping to conclusions is one of the poorest forms of exercise, and it's a sure way to stumble. When Senator Dan Inouye of Hawaii was sworn into office, he raised his left hand instead of the customary right hand. A vicious critic noted this quickly and publicly. But the critic did not know the whole story: Senator Inouye lost his right arm defending the United States in World War II.

Next time you're tempted to make a quick judgment of someone, try giving people the benefit of the doubt instead. An old Puritan preacher once said that God wanted us to watch our words so much that he put our tongue behind two barriers: our lips and our teeth.

"I whomped one with an ax handle. I choked another one till he died. I squished 'em all!"

Chapter 21

RAT RAID

Babies are born without guile. They cry, sleep, eat, and mess up their diapers without any worry about what people think. But kids soon begin to take up the bad adult habit of pretending to be something they're not; they start playing roles, and they learn most of those roles from us. If Mom puts on her makeup a certain way, so will Sis. If Dad walks with a certain gait, so will Junior. Scientists have even found that monkeys in a zoo will imitate human expressions in order to get peanuts.

We had a lot of good times growing up out in the country with my grandma and my grandpa. Among other small-town rituals we observed, we were faithful to attend church every week. I learned the "churchy" ways early and tried to mind my manners at church. I soon realized it was almost as if you

had one life when you were away from church and another
when you were at church. On church days, you were a little
more pious, and you put on your little halo, making sure it was
all shined up.

I heard a story once about another little boy who was raised
out there in the country. He was just a regular little boy, and he
liked to play out in the barn. One day he found a whole nest of
rats there.

He was so excited. "Oh, boy! Lord help me, I'm gonna get
'em."

He killed every single one of those rats. He was so proud of
what he had done; he felt like a hero. Full of enthusiasm, he ran
back to the house to show off those dead rats. He didn't know
that the preacher was there, making a visit.

He burst into the house, happily holding those dead rats,
and declared, "Mama, Daddy, you'll be so proud of me. I
found a nest of those big old rats, and I got 'em! I whomped up
on 'em good with an ax handle. And Daddy, I grabbed one,
and I choked him till he died. I squished 'em all. I stomped on
'em, and now they're all dead!"

Of course, Mama was shrieking, "Eeeee!"

And Dad was moaning, "Oh, no."

Then the little boy saw the preacher sitting in the corner. All
of a sudden, he became very solemn and said, "And then, Pastor, God called them home."

Isn't that the way we all are? We're sort of trained to sound

a certain way when certain people are looking. This is often true of preachers and other spiritual leaders.

FOOD FOR THOUGHT

Servants, obey in all things your masters according to the flesh, not with eye-service, as men-pleasers, but in sincerity of heart, fearing God.

—Colossians 3:22

Paul was very proud of the Philippian church because the members were always the same, regardless of who was around. He commended them for their steadfastness: "My beloved, as you have always obeyed, not as in my presence only, but now much more in my absence, work out your own salvation with fear and trembling; for it is God who works in you both to will and to do for His good pleasure" (2:12–13).

Paul had been gone from the Greek city of Philippi for ten years. Although he had not been in the presence of those believers for a decade, he was proud of them because they were more eager to please God in Paul's absence than his presence. Why? Because they truly believed the Lord Jesus Christ was present with them at all times.

We Christians are a curious sort. If we think a preacher or another dedicated Christian is nearby, we clean up our act. But if no one is watching, we let loose. Don't we know that God is always there? Even though he is unseen, God is more real than any other person around you.

The story is told that one day Billy Graham was playing golf with a famous president. When the president was unhappy with one of his shots, he turned the air blue with four-letter words. Then he abjectly apologized to Graham.

Graham told him, "You don't owe *me* an apology. God is always there."

The all-pro defensive end for the Cleveland Browns, Bill Glass, put it this way: Sometimes he would make a play that pleased the crowd and brought cheers of excitement, but he knew that if he had made the play from the wrong position, his coach would not be pleased. Glass learned early in his professional career that he was playing to please just one person—the coach. He was not playing to please the crowd or even his fellow team members. He later observed that, in the same way, we Christians should play the game of life to please only one Person, the Lord Jesus Christ.

Who we really are is who we are when only God is watching us. When we are in a strange city, all alone, with only our own identity below and God above, that's who we really are. Let's be true to that identity. We don't have to play games anymore.

*"Dear God, thank you
for my praline. Amen."*

CINDY'S PRALINE

George Mueller stands out as a towering example of prayer for all times. Mueller operated an orphanage in Bristol, England, in the nineteenth century. Yet he did it in a way that shocked even the most dedicated believers. Mueller never asked any person on earth for help. He provided for the orphanage simply by asking God to supply their needs. The dramatic answers to his prayers are well documented.

One evening Mueller learned that there was no food for the next day. Sorely tempted to ask for human help, Mueller instead called the entire orphanage to prayer. Together they asked God to supply their needs for food the next day. The following morning, a bread truck literally broke down at the door of the orphanage. With no way to transport the bread, the driver knocked on the door and offered it to Mueller.

George Mueller's life was filled with such episodes. What would our lives be like if we trusted God with an equally child-like faith? How would our days be different if we believed that absolutely nothing is too great for God's power or too small for his attention? The experience of a good friend's family was like that.

After I became a Christian, I attended a Baptist church in Austin where Marshall Edwards was the pastor. Marshall was the chaplain for my football team at Reagan High School—the state champions three out of the four years I played. Marshall was a super guy who motivated us before every football game. He was so loved by the athletes and the student body that we nicknamed him "Rabbi." I loved the "Rabbi"; his wife, Doris; his son, Scott; and his little girl, Cindy.

Like all ministers of the gospel, Marshall loved Mexican food. One night, Marshall, Doris, and little Cindy went out to El Chico's Tex-Mex restaurant. They enjoyed their meal and their time together. As they were at the register paying the check, Marshall decided that he would get Doris, Cindy, and himself each a praline for dessert.

They got into their Ford LTD—the minister's answer to a Cadillac—and as they were driving off, little Cindy, sitting in the backseat of the car, started talking to herself like four-year-old girls often do.

She said, "Cindy, you haven't had a praline in a long time."

When Cindy said that, Doris sort of teared up. Marshall

loved it too. They continued to listen as she said, "I think I'll pray for my praline."

Tears were now flowing down Doris's cheeks, and even Marshall's eyes were getting misty.

Cindy began to pray, "Dear God, thank you for my praline. Amen."

Marshall and Doris were both so proud and full of love for their little girl. Then they heard something they hadn't expected to hear.

Little Cindy lowered her voice and said, "You're welcome, Cindy."

I haven't had quite that unique a relationship with the Lord. However, little Cindy, in her heart of hearts, was genuinely talking to God. I'm sure she did hear that still, small voice that is louder than any audible voice. It is the voice of God, which speaks to the heart and responds to the prayers of those who have a childlike faith.

Does God care whether a little girl gets a praline? You bet. God loves to provide for his children. And he loves to provide for our major needs as well as for the minor details of everyday life.

Food for Thought

My God shall supply all your need according to His riches in glory by Christ Jesus.

—Philippians 4:19

One of history's great prayer warriors was the famous preacher Charles H. Spurgeon. His wife, Susannah, was ill and was confined to their London home during much of the great pastor's ministry. Charles often had to catch a train to go off and preach, and Susannah usually sent him off with something silly or humorous, just to lighten the load of their separation.

In his autobiography, Charles recorded that one day as he was leaving for an extended trip, Susannah teased, "Please bring back a piping bullfinch and an opal ring."

On the train trip to his destination, Charles sat next to a person who recognized him. After all, Charles Spurgeon was one of the most famous men in Victorian England. The person offered him a gift for Mrs. Spurgeon. From a jewelry box, the passenger handed him an opal ring!

That is astounding enough. But there's more. When Charles arrived at his destination, his hostess had a birdcage with— you guessed it—a piping bullfinch. When Spurgeon told his hostess of the incredible "coincidence," she insisted that he take the bird with him as a present for his wife.

Don't be afraid to ask your heavenly Father for anything you need. Indeed, nothing is too small for God's attention or too great for his power.

Ron's mom feverishly responded with a big smile and quickly moving hands. She signed, "I love you in Jesus!"

Chapter 23

HAIRNETS AND HALOS

My buddy Ron Harris has a mama just like mine. She is submissive, loving, innocent, and naive. Ona Mae is a sweetheart who loves Jesus and his people. No one's a stranger long around Ron's mama.

One afternoon, Ona Mae, Ron, and his wife, Judy, were standing on the corner of a busy intersection adjacent to a mall and strip shopping center. While waiting for the light to change, Ona Mae noticed a young lady across the street using sign language. As she had learned a bit of sign language in church training, she couldn't let the opportunity pass.

Immediately Ona Mae tried to get the young lady's attention and signed the letters for "I love you in Jesus." She was so proud of her ability to communicate. But the lady across the

Chapter Twenty-Three

street ignored Ona Mae's message and just continued to sign. Ona Mae wasn't very fluent in sign language, so she couldn't discern what the lady was signing. Undaunted, she once again tried to get the young lady's attention, repeating her message in sign language, sharing the gospel as simply as she knew how.

Ron and Judy were a little embarrassed but intrigued with Ona Mae's desire to witness to this young lady. When the light changed, they began walking toward one another. The young lady from across the street continued to sign, and Ron's mom feverishly responded with a big smile and quickly moving hands. She signed again, "I love you in Jesus!"

In the middle of the street, Ona Mae finally met her new friend, only to discover that the young lady wasn't signing at all but was trying to untangle her hairnet!

A quick conversation revealed that the young lady worked at a nearby cafeteria. When everyone involved realized what had happened, they burst into laugher and helped untangle the hairnet. All the while, Ona Mae did her best to explain the gospel to the young cafeteria worker, but this time not in sign language.

FOOD FOR THOUGHT

Preach the word! Be ready in season and out of season.
—2 Timothy 4:2

There are times when it is tough to get the message through. When the Duke of Wellington of Great Britain was fighting

Napoleon of France at Waterloo, the whole of Western civilization stood in the balance. All of England held its breath. If Napoleon could not be stopped, England would soon become part of Napoleon's expanding empire.

Fortunately, the Duke of Wellington won the battle, and a famous smoke signal was transmitted back to England. It said: "Wellington defeated . . ." Then the signal was interrupted by a sudden fog. England was thrown into turmoil, thinking that their army had lost the battle.

Finally, the fog lifted and the remainder of the message could be seen: "Wellington defeated Napoleon." One word made all the difference to the people of England.

When our Lord Jesus Christ died on the cross, one word made all the difference to every person for all time. Just before he died, Jesus cried out, "It is finished" (John 19:30).

He did not say, "I am finished." That would have meant the end of him.

He did not say, "You are finished." That would have meant the end of us.

He cried out in victory that the great plan of God to save humans was finished. With one word, Jesus Christ defeated the schemes of Satan for all eternity. That message has come through clearly for two thousand years.

Ron noticed more than a hairnet that afternoon. He also saw the halo over his mother's head. Ona Mae was faithful in season and out of season. In doing her best for the Lord, she was trying to learn someone else's language to communicate the all-important gospel of our Lord and Savior Jesus Christ.

Never underestimate the power of any witness. On the street that day there was something other than hairnets and halos. A gospel seed was planted that may have been the beginning of a new soul added to the kingdom. God knows that even hairnets can be used to open the door for witness.

Praise God for hairnets and halos and sweet little ladies like Ona Mae Harris. May we never stop witnessing with our testimonies, with our hands, with our preaching, and with our lifestyles.

"Please sing 'Jingle Bells.'
It was his favorite song.
Sing it with all your heart,
soul, and mind."

Chapter 24

A GRAVESIDE JINGLE

The work of the Lord is sometimes called the "ministry of messes" because it is so easy for ministers to mess up. Nevertheless, we preachers give it our best. We give it all for Jesus. And occasionally, we fumble—hopefully not on the goal line, but it does happen.

In one small country church, the pastor and associate pastor were both out of town. That left Zach, the church's minister of education, in charge. While the two pastors were away, a parishioner passed on to glory. Zach made his way to the home of Ma and Pa Bell. Pa had gone on to be with the Lord, and Zach found Ma Bell sobbing. She and her husband had journeyed together for more than fifty years.

Coming to the rescue, Zach embraced Ma Bell, and they

cried together. Everyone had loved Pa Bell. He'd been a patri-
arch in north Mississippi. Every hill and glen had reaped a
blessing from Pa Bell. He was the salt of the earth. He had a
great sense of humor and was the life of the party.

Ma calmed down a bit, looked into Zach's eyes, and asked,
"Zach, will you do Pa's funeral?"

"Well," said Zach, "I'm not a preacher, and I don't know
any of that fancy talkin'. But if you want me to, I'll do my best."

"Pa loved you, Zach. You have been with us on our senior
trips to Branson, Chataguas, and the Grand Ol' Opry, not to
mention the Christmas parties you planned each year. I know
Pa would be pleased to have you do his graveside service."

"Graveside?" Zach repeated.

"Yes, Pa wanted a small funeral for family members only in
the country at the cemetery."

"But, Ma," Zach protested. "Everybody loved Pa. We could
pack out the church sanctuary."

"I know that, Zach," she said as the tears began to flow
again. "But I'm going to honor his request."

With a hanky in each hand, Ma continued, "Zach, would
you also sing at the graveside service?"

Zach gasped, "But, Ma, I'm not really a singer."

"I know, Zach, but you lead the music for our teenagers. I
really want you to sing," she said between sobs. "It will just be
me, our three boys with their families, and about a dozen close
friends," wept Ma. "Please sing for us."

"Well, I guess I can do it," said Zach.

162

☾ A Graveside Jingle ☾

"Good," said Ma. "I want you to sing Pa's favorite song," she said as her emotions built even further. "I want you to sing 'Jingle Bells.'"

Did I hear her right? thought Zach. "Did you say 'Jingle Bells'?"

"Yes," she said, sobbing uncontrollably. "Please sing 'Jingle Bells.' It was his favorite song, and he requested it. Sing it with all your heart, soul, and mind, Zach. Please, Zach, for me, for Pa, and for Jesus."

I know that we are to become all things to all people so that we might win some, but "Jingle Bells"! thought Zach. *This will be a first and, prayerfully, a last.*

On the appointed day, the family approached the cemetery. Zach rode with the funeral director and Pa's coffin. Zach had already shared his heart with Pa, vowing that he would get even with him in heaven.

Zach looked right at that coffin and told Pa, "I'm going to ask Jesus to have you sing 'Jingle Bells' right before the judgment seat of Christ!"

They drove down cemetery row. Ol' Digger (that's really his name) had already moved the backhoe out of the way. The six-car processional came to a stop in front of the green tent. The flowers and potted plants on the grave site looked beautiful.

I still say we should have had his funeral at the church, but perhaps God is watching out for me, thought Zach.

He looked at the program. "Jingle Bells" was still on the order of worship.

At least my wife and children aren't here to hear this, mused Zach.

Everyone stood under the tent, sobbing. Pa Bell was sorely missed. Finally the funeral director nodded, indicating it was time to begin the service. Zach prayed, read some Scripture, and then began: "I want to sing a song that Pa loved. It might seem a bit unusual to some of you, but the family knows how much Pa loved Christmas. He loved the season celebrating our Lord and Savior's birth. So I want to sing this simple song that was Pa's favorite."

Slowly and softer than usual, he sang, "Jingle bells, jingle bells, jingle all the way. Oh, what fun. . . . "

Ma Bell gasped and threw her hands into the air. Zach tried hard to keep a reverence to his new rendition of "Jingle Bells."

But Ma Bell cried out, "Oh, Zach, I'm sorry! It's not 'Jingle Bells,' it's 'When They Ring Those Golden Bells'!"

Poor Zach stripped what gears he had as he changed keys and went right into the refrain, "When they ring those golden bells for you and me."

Although Ma Bell laughed through her tears, Zach looked as white as a sheet. The family thought he was going to join Pa right then and there. Everyone gathered around poor old Zach and laughed, cried, and laughed some more.

Zach decided to stick with education ministry from that moment on. But he was loved and appreciated by Pa's family. The Lord must have a sense of humor.

Ol' Digger believes to this day that you can hear those bells at that cemetery.

 *A Graveside Jingle*

I'm so glad death is swallowed up in victory. Our sorrow is but for a little while, for a better day is coming. We can rejoice when a fellow believer makes his way to his heavenly home.

FOOD FOR THOUGHT
Death is swallowed up in victory.
—1 Corinthians 15:54

The Lord Jesus really has changed what we can sing and say at the graveside. The apostle Paul once imagined himself standing by an open grave, that gash in the soul of the earth, and heard himself crying out in mockery of what death has done: "'O Death, where is your sting? O Hades, where is your victory?' The sting of death is sin, and the strength of sin is the law. But thanks be to God, who gives us the victory through our Lord Jesus Christ" (1 Corinthians 15:55–57).

Paul can mock the very worst things death can do because he knows the Victor over death. We have the promise that because he lives, we shall live also.

Walter Loudermilk was a great conservationist and professor at the University of California at Berkeley. He was also a Christian. As a young married couple, he and his wife, Inez, found some uprooted yucca plants in the desert alongside the road. They placed them in their car, returned to their Bay area home, and planted them in their backyard. For decades the plants did not bloom, as yucca plants bloom only once.

The day came when the doctor told the Loudermilks that the scientist's days were numbered. As if by the finger of God, the yucca plant that had not bloomed for many years suddenly began to grow, almost a foot a day at its stalk. Then, on the very day that Loudermilk died, the stalk burst into full bloom. In *Guideposts* magazine, his family shared how they saw this as a sign of God's victory over death. Out of the apparent death of the yucca, saved many years ago, suddenly came life.

So it is with the resurrection of the dead in Christ. I'm looking forward to the day when God "rings those golden bells" for you and me.

Chapter 25

WEEPING, WAILING, AND GNASHING OF TEETH

As a minister of the gospel for more than twenty years, I have always enjoyed opportunities to fellowship with other preachers. I love to spend time with preachers from every kind of background: the highly educated and people-oriented pastor; the shepherd who tends a flock of ten or twenty; the crusty old country preacher who rants and raves; and the quiet, sophisticated pastor. They are all special and precious in God's sight. And, like me, all of them are very human.

In the old days, we seemed to do more preaching on heaven and hell. There are a lot of folks who feel that there was too much fire-and-brimstone preached back then. Nowadays we don't hear much about the fire-and-brimstone because we are afraid to preach about hell, which is probably an injustice to the brethren.

This fact is even more interesting in light of how often we hear the word *hell* used as an expletive in daily conversation. Why do you suppose people use that word so much? Could it be the outward expression of their real inward feeling? People say "Oh, hell" because that is what they feel. Let me suggest an experiment. Get on a crowded elevator and simply cry out "Oh, heaven!" When the doors open and people are getting off the elevator, cry out "Heaven!" again. It'll sure get folks' attention because they're used to hearin' about the other place a whole lot more.

I remember the story of an old country preacher who was preaching his heart out one evening. He was preaching the last sermon in a series on hell. The people had heard messages on hell for at least a month. At the peak of this sermon, he yelled out to the congregation, "And in hell there will be weeping and wailing and gnashing of teeth!" You could have heard a pin drop.

He said, "Did you hear me? There will be weeping and wailing and gnashing of teeth!"

Folks were doing some heavy breathing.

Then he said it a third time for emphasis, "There will be weeping and wailing and gnashing of teeth!"

A country farmer in his overalls attended church on occasion out of respect for his wife and family even though he was an unbeliever and a skeptic. He decided to have a little fun with the preacher, so he looked up and said, without a tooth in his head, "But, Preacher, what if you ain't got no teeth?"

A hush settled over the congregation.

The preacher responded with great solemnity, "Teeth will be provided."

I'm not exactly sure what hell is like. I don't know whether it's a place of darkness, a lake of fire, or a land of weeping, wailing, and gnashing of teeth (with teeth provided). But I do know this much. Hell is separation from a loving God. It is a place that God does not intend for any of us to go. It has not been prepared for his children, though it is a place to which one can choose to go. It is my prayer that we would all choose to be with Christ in heaven instead. Sink your teeth into that message.

FOOD FOR THOUGHT

*Our citizenship is in heaven, from which we also eagerly
wait for the Savior, the Lord Jesus Christ.*

—Philippians 3:20

One of the greatest lay theologians of this century was C. S. Lewis, author of many books for children and adults. In *The Great Divorce,* one of his most unusual books, the word *divorce* does not refer to marriage but to the great separation between heaven and hell. A group of folks decides to take a bus trip from hell to heaven. First of all, it's hard to get them all together. Rather than being a crowded place, hell is a place where people live at incredible distances from one another.

When they do get together, nobody can get along with anybody else. It's a long trip to heaven.

When the bus finally gets to heaven, the real problems begin. The light in heaven is too bright for their eyes. The water in heaven is so substantial that they can walk on it but not drink it, so they cannot satisfy their thirst. They watch the citizens of heaven drink the water and wonder why it is too thick for them to drink. The grass in heaven feels like spikes beneath their feet, even though it is soft to the citizens of heaven.

The brilliant point made by Lewis is this: Heaven is ultimate reality; hell is ultimate nonreality. Yes, hell is a real place with eternal consequences for the people who have chosen to be there. But hell is an *unreal* place for people who never got *real* about the Lord Jesus Christ. Lewis contends that such people could never stand heaven even if they got there.

Makes you wonder, why would someone who couldn't stand an hour on Sunday praisin' God on Earth want to spend forever and ever doing nothing but praisin' God in a service with no benediction in heaven? That would be hell to them.

Heaven is a place Christians can practice for. Prayer, praise, congregational worship, and fellowship will tune you up for the Big Forever. What the heaven! I can't wait.

Videos/CDs/Audios
  Loosen Up, Laugh, and Live
  Back to Back with Laughter
  Is Your Love Tank Full?
  Laughter from the Rafters
  Planting Shade Trees
  Smiling with the Saints
  Christmas with the Swan
  Life on the Lighter Side
  Baseball, Buffets, and a Barrel of Laughs
  A View from the Blimp (video only)
  Best of Swan's Place (video only)

Books
  Is Your Love Tank Full, or Are You Loving on Empty?
  Swan's Soup & Salad
  Why A.D.H.D. Doesn't Mean Disaster

For bookings, products, and ministry, please contact:

Swanberg Christian Ministries
PO Box 1495
West Monroe, LA 71294
318-325-9044 • fax: 318-325-0012
Web site: www.denisswanberg.com

Printed in the United States
By Bookmasters